Careers in Focus

CLERKS AND ADMINISTRATIVE WORKERS

SECOND EDITION

Ferguson
An imprint of Infobase Publishing

Careers in Focus: Clerks and Administrative Workers, Second Edition

Copyright © 2010 by Infobase Publishing

Ferguson
An imprint of Infobase Publishing
132 West 31st Street
New York NY 10001

Library of Congress Cataloging-in-Publication Data

Careers in focus. Clerks and administrative workers. — 2nd ed.
    p. cm.
Includes bibliographical references and index.
ISBN-13: 978-0-8160-8017-5 (hardcover : alk. paper)
ISBN-10: 0-8160-8017-8 (hardcover : alk. paper) 1. Clerical occupations—Juvenile literature. I. Ferguson Publishing.
HF5547.5.C335 2010
651.3'702373—dc22
                                    2009044720

Ferguson books are available at special discounts when purchased in bulk quantities for businesses, associations, institutions, or sales promotions. Please call our Special Sales Department in New York at (212) 967-8800 or (800) 322-8755.

You can find Ferguson on the World Wide Web at http://www.fergpubco.com

Text design by David Strelecky
Cover design by Takeshi Takahashi
Composition by Mary Susan Ryan-Flynn
Cover printed by Art Print Company, Taylor, PA
Book printed and bound by Maple Press, York, PA
Date printed: May 2010
Printed in the United States of America

10 9 8 7 6 5 4 3 2 1

This book is printed on acid-free paper.

Table of Contents

Introduction 1

Billing Clerks 5

Bookkeeping and Accounting Clerks 11

Collection Workers 18

Counter and Retail Clerks 25

Financial Institution Tellers, Clerks,
    and Related Workers 31

Hotel Desk Clerks 42

Insurance Policy Processing Workers 50

Legal Secretaries 57

Library Technicians 67

Medical Record Technicians 79

Medical Secretaries 90

Medical Transcriptionists 95

Office Clerks 105

Railroad Clerks 111

Real Estate Clerks 118

Receptionists 124

Secretaries 131

Statistical Clerks 140

Stock Clerks 146

Typists and Word Processors 153

Index 161

Introduction

Clerks and administrative workers are employed in a wide variety of work environments, from grocery stores and collection agencies to corporate law firms and executive offices. Their duties range from general bookkeeping, typing, and office tasks to more specialized tasks such as medical transcription and insurance policy processing. Many different types of employers hire secretaries and administrative workers, and these employees have varied levels of responsibility depending on the size of the firm, business, or institution. There are more than 4.2 million secretaries and administrative assistants employed throughout the United States, as well as 1.2 million receptionists and information clerks, making this field one of the country's largest. Approximately 90 percent of secretaries and administrative assistants work in service industries.

Administrative work is often entry level; many employees use their experience as a stepping-stone to more advanced positions. However, a considerable number of clerks and administrative workers remain in this field, with a growing number advancing to positions of higher responsibility. In fact, 73 percent of managers surveyed in 2008 by OfficeTeam reported that the responsibilities of their support workers had increased "significantly" or "somewhat" in the past five years. The added responsibilities have translated into improved career opportunities for many administrative workers. Fifty-seven percent of survey respondents believed that administrative workers had more of an advancement track than they had five years earlier.

Clerks and administrative workers must be able to interact with all different kinds of people, and they must be computer literate. These workers must also be organized, attentive, and able to follow directions. The secretary or receptionist is often the first person that a client sees, so a professional appearance and friendly demeanor are a must for workers in this field. Clerks and administrative workers should be detail-oriented and have patience to complete repetitive tasks.

In recent years, advances in technology have revolutionized traditional secretarial tasks such as typing or keeping records of correspondence. The use of email, scanners, database programs, and the Internet has had a major impact on this field and will continue to do so in years to come.

As a whole, clerks and administrative workers are expected to experience average employment growth over the next several years. However, several careers in this field have experienced better than average growth in recent years. For example, the U.S. Department of Labor projects that employment for medical transcriptionists will grow by approximately 14 percent from 2006 to 2016, which is faster than the national average for all occupations. As the population ages and grows, more medical services are required by the elderly, which has also increased the need for medical secretaries and medical record technicians. Strong employment growth is also predicted for collection workers, counter and retail clerks, hotel desk clerks, and receptionists.

The articles in *Careers in Focus: Clerks and Administrative Workers* appear in Ferguson's *Encyclopedia of Careers and Vocational Guidance,* but have been updated and revised with the latest information from the U.S. Department of Labor, professional organizations, and other sources.

The following paragraphs detail the sections and features that appear in the book.

The **Quick Facts** section provides a brief summary of the career, including recommended school subjects, personal skills, work environment, minimum educational requirements, salary ranges, certification or licensing requirements, and employment outlook. This section also provides acronyms and identification numbers for the following government classification indexes: the Dictionary of Occupational Titles (DOT), the Guide for Occupational Exploration (GOE), the National Occupational Classification (NOC) Index, and the Occupational Information Network (O*NET)-Standard Occupational Classification System (SOC) index. The DOT, GOE, and O*NET-SOC indexes have been created by the U.S. government; the NOC index is Canada's career-classification system. Readers can use the identification numbers listed in the Quick Facts section to access further information about a career. Print editions of the DOT (*Dictionary of Occupational Titles.* Indianapolis, Ind.: JIST Works, 1991) and GOE (*Guide for Occupational Exploration.* Indianapolis, Ind.: JIST Works, 2001) are available at libraries. Versions of the NOC (http://www.hrsdc.gc.ca/eng/workplaceskills/noc/index.shtml) and O*NET-SOC (http://online.onetcenter.org) are available online. When no DOT, GOE, NOC, or O*NET-SOC numbers are present, this means that the U.S. Department of Labor or Human Resources Development Canada have not created a numerical designation for this career. In this instance, you will see the acronym "N/A," or not available.

The **Overview** section is a brief introductory description of the duties and responsibilities of this career. Oftentimes, a career may have a variety of job titles. When this is the case, alternative career titles are presented. Employment statistics are also provided, when available. The **History** section describes the history of the particular job as it relates to the overall development of its industry or field. **The Job** describes the primary and secondary duties of the job. **Requirements** discusses high school and postsecondary education and training requirements, any certification or licensing that is necessary, and other personal requirements for success in the job. **Exploring** offers suggestions on how to gain experience in or knowledge of the particular job before making a firm educational and financial commitment. The focus is on what can be done while still in high school (or in the early years of college) to gain a better understanding of the job. The **Employers** section gives an overview of typical places of employment for the job. **Starting Out** discusses the best ways to land that first job, be it through the college career services office, newspaper ads, Internet employment sites, or a personal contact. The **Advancement** section describes what kind of career path to expect from the job and how to get there. **Earnings** lists salary ranges and describes the typical fringe benefits. The **Work Environment** section describes the typical surroundings and conditions of employment—whether indoors or outdoors, noisy or quiet, social or independent. Also discussed are typical hours worked, any seasonal fluctuations, and the stresses and strains of the job. The **Outlook** section summarizes the job in terms of the general economy and industry projections. For the most part, Outlook information is obtained from the U.S. Bureau of Labor Statistics and is supplemented by information gathered from professional associations. Job growth terms follow those used in the *Occupational Outlook Handbook*. Growth described as "much faster than the average" means an increase of 21 percent or more. Growth described as "faster than the average" means an increase of 14 to 20 percent. Growth described as "about as fast as the average" means an increase of 7 to 13 percent. Growth described as "more slowly than the average" means an increase of 3 to 6 percent. "Little or no change" means a decrease of 2 percent to an increase of 2 percent. "Decline" means a decrease of 3 percent or more. Each article ends with **For More Information,** which lists organizations that provide information on training, education, internships, scholarships, and job placement.

Careers in Focus: Clerks and Administrative Workers also includes photographs, informative sidebars, and interviews with professionals in the field.

The field of clerical and administrative work offers a wide variety of opportunities to suit many different interests. This book provides a comprehensive overview of these careers and abundant information to help you prepare for work of this nature.

Billing Clerks

OVERVIEW

Billing clerks produce and process bills and collect payments from customers. They enter transactions in business ledgers or spreadsheets, write and send invoices, and verify purchase orders. They post items in accounts payable or receivable, calculate customer charges, and verify the company's rates for certain products and services. Billing clerks must make sure that all entries are accurate and up-to-date. At the end of the fiscal year, they may work with auditors to clarify billing procedures and answer questions about specific accounts. There are approximately 542,000 billing clerks employed in the United States.

HISTORY

The need to record business transactions has existed ever since people began to engage in business and commerce. As far back as 3000 B.C., Sumerians in Mesopotamia recorded sales and bills for customers on clay tablets. Wealthy traders of early Egyptian and Babylonian civilizations often used slaves to make markings on clay tablets to keep track of purchases and sales.

With the rise of monarchies in Europe, billing clerks were needed to record the business transactions of kings, queens, and rich merchants and to monitor the status of the royal treasury. During the Middle Ages, monks carried out the tasks of billing clerks. As the industrial revolution spread across Europe and commercial transactions increased, billing clerks became a necessary part of the workforce.

Computer technology has changed the way clerks record transactions today, eliminating paperwork and allowing billing information and financial transactions to be recorded electronically. But billing clerks continue to occupy a central role in the business world, managing the day-to-day inner workings of company finance.

THE JOB

Billing clerks are responsible for keeping up-to-date records of all business transactions. They type and send bills for services or products and update files to reflect payments. They also review incoming invoices to ensure that the requested products have been delivered and that the billing statements are accurate and paid on time.

Billing clerks set up shipping and receiving dates. They check customer orders before shipping to make sure they are complete and that all costs, shipping charges, taxes, and credits are included. Billing clerks are also troubleshooters. They contact suppliers or customers when payments are past due or incorrect and help solve the minor problems that invariably occur in the course of business transactions.

Billing clerks enter all transaction information into the firm's account ledger. This ledger lists all the company's transactions, such as items bought or sold, credit terms, and payment and receiving dates. As payments come in, the billing clerk applies credit to customer accounts and applies any applicable discounts. All correspondence is carefully filed for future reference. Nearly all of this work is done using spreadsheets and computer databases.

The specific duties of billing clerks vary according to the nature of the business in which they work. In an insurance company, the transaction sheet will reflect when and how much customers must pay on their insurance bills. Billing clerks in hospitals compile itemized charges, calculate insurance benefits, and process insurance claims. In accounting, law, and consulting firms, they calculate billable hours and work completed.

Billing clerks are also often responsible for preparing summary statements of financial status, profit-and-loss statements, and payroll lists and deductions. These reports are submitted periodically to company management, who can then gauge the company's financial performance. Clerks may also write company checks, compute federal tax reports, and tabulate personnel profit shares.

Billing clerks may have a specific role within a company. These areas of specialization include the following:

Invoice-control clerks post items in accounts payable or receivable ledgers and verify the accuracy of billing data.

Passenger rate clerks compute fare information for business trips and then provide this information to business personnel.

COD (cash-on-delivery) clerks calculate and record the amount of money collected on COD delivery routes.

Interline clerks compute and pay freight charges for airlines or other transportation agencies that carry freight or passengers as part of a business transaction.

Settlement clerks compute and pay shippers for materials forwarded to a company.

Billing-control clerks compute and pay utility companies for services provided.

Rate reviewers compile data relating to utility costs for management officials.

Services clerks compute and pay tariff charges for boats or ships used to transport materials.

Foreign clerks compute duties, tariffs, and price conversions of exported and imported products.

Billing-machine operators mechanically prepare bills and statements.

Deposit-refund clerks prepare bills for utility customers.

Raters calculate premiums to be paid by customers of insurance companies.

Telegraph-service raters compute costs for sending telegrams.

Billing clerks may work in one specific area or they may be responsible for several areas.

REQUIREMENTS

High School
A high school diploma is usually sufficient for a beginning billing clerk, although business courses in computer operations and bookkeeping are also helpful. In high school, take English, communications, and business writing courses. Computer science and mathematics courses will also prepare you for this career. Some companies test their applicants on math, typing, and computer skills, and others offer on-the-job training.

Postsecondary Training
Community colleges, junior colleges, and vocational schools often offer business education courses that can provide you with additional training.

Other Requirements

If you hope to be a billing clerk, you should have excellent mathematical and organizational skills, be detail oriented, and be able to concentrate on repetitive tasks for long periods of time. In addition, you should be dependable, honest, and trustworthy in dealing with confidential financial matters.

EXPLORING

You can gain experience in this field by taking on clerical or bookkeeping responsibilities with a school club, student government, or other extracurricular activities. If you are interested in the field, you can work in retail operations, either part time or during the summer. Working at the cash register or even pricing products as a stockperson is a good introductory experience. It also may be possible to gain some experience by volunteering to help maintain the bookkeeping records for local groups, such as churches and small businesses.

EMPLOYERS

Employers of billing clerks include hospitals, insurance companies, banks, manufacturers, and utility companies. Of the approximately 542,000 billing clerks employed in the United States, more than one-third work in the health care field. Wholesale and resale trade industries also employ a large number of billing clerks. Businesses that provide billing services for other companies employ about 11 percent of these workers—mainly in the accounting, administrative and support services, bookkeeping, payroll services, and tax preparation industries. Approximately 16 percent of billing clerks work part time.

STARTING OUT

Your high school job placement or guidance office can help you find employment opportunities or establish job contacts after you graduate. You may also find specific jobs through classified newspaper advertisements. Most companies provide on-the-job training for entry-level billing clerks to explain to them company procedures and policies and to teach them the basic tasks of the job. During the first month, billing clerks work with experienced personnel.

ADVANCEMENT

Billing clerks usually begin by handling routine tasks such as recording transactions. With experience, they may advance to more complex assignments—which entail computer training in databases and spreadsheets—and assume a greater responsibility for the work as a whole. With additional training and education, billing clerks can be promoted to positions as bookkeepers, accountants, or auditors. Billing clerks with strong leadership and management skills can advance to group manager or supervisor.

There is a high turnover rate in this field, which increases the chance of promotion for employees with ability and initiative.

EARNINGS

Salaries for billing clerks depend on the size and geographic location of the company and the employee's skills. Staring salaries for an employee with little experience may be around $20,000 a year. Full-time billing and posting clerks earned a median hourly wage of $14.41 in 2007, according to the U.S. Department of Labor. For full-time work at 40 hours per week, this hourly wage translates into an annual income of approximately $29,970. Some bill and account collectors may earn a commission based on the number of cases they close in a given time period. Billing clerks with high levels of expertise and management responsibilities may make $43,160 a year or more. Full-time workers also receive paid vacation, health insurance, and other benefits.

WORK ENVIRONMENT

Like most office workers, billing clerks usually work in modern office environments and average 40 hours of work per week. Billing clerks spend most of their time behind a desk, and their work can be routine and repetitive. Working long hours in front of a computer can often cause eyestrain, backaches, and headaches, although efforts are being made to reduce physical problems with ergonomically correct equipment. Billing clerks should enjoy systematic and orderly work and have a keen eye for numerical detail. While much of the work is solitary, billing clerks often interact with accountants and management and may work under close supervision.

OUTLOOK

The U.S. Department of Labor predicts that employment for billing clerks will grow more slowly than the average for all careers through 2016. A number of factors will contribute to this slow growth rate. For example, technological advancements—computers, electronic billing, and automated payment methods—will streamline operations and result in the need for fewer workers. The rising popularity of billing via the Internet will also eliminate the number of billing clerks needed in many businesses. Additionally, the responsibilities of billing clerks may be combined with those of other positions. In smaller companies, for example, accounting clerks will make use of billing software, making billing clerks obsolete. Many job openings will result from the need to replace workers who have left for different jobs or other reasons. The health care sector should remain a large employer in this field.

FOR MORE INFORMATION

For information on union membership, contact
Office and Professional Employees International Union
265 West 14th Street, 6th Floor
New York, NY 10011-7103
Tel: 800-346-7348
http://www.opeiu.org

For free office career and salary information, visit the following Web site:
OfficeTeam
http://www.officeteam.com

Bookkeeping and Accounting Clerks

OVERVIEW

Bookkeeping and accounting clerks record financial transactions for government, business, and other organizations. They compute, classify, record, and verify numerical data in order to develop and maintain accurate financial records. There are approximately 2.1 million bookkeeping, accounting, and auditing clerks employed in the United States.

HISTORY

The history of bookkeeping developed along with the growth of business and industrial enterprise. The first known records of bookkeeping date back to 2600 B.C., when the Babylonians used pointed sticks to mark accounts on clay slabs. By 3000 B.C., Middle Eastern and Egyptian cultures employed a system of numbers to record merchants' transactions of the grain and farm products that were distributed from storage warehouses. The growth of intricate trade systems brought about the necessity for bookkeeping systems.

Sometime after the start of the 13th century, the decimal numeration system was introduced in Europe, simplifying bookkeeping record systems. The merchants of Venice—one of the busiest trading centers in the world at that time—are credited with the invention of the double entry bookkeeping method that is widely used today.

As industry in the United States expands and grows more complex, simpler and quicker bookkeeping methods and procedures have evolved. Technological developments include bookkeeping machines, computer hardware and software, and electronic data processing.

THE JOB

Bookkeeping workers keep systematic records and current accounts of financial transactions for businesses, institutions, industries, charities, and other organizations. The bookkeeping records of a firm or business are a vital part of its operational procedures because these records reflect the assets and the liabilities, as well as the profits and losses, of the operation.

Bookkeepers record these business transactions daily in spreadsheets on computer databases, and accounting clerks often input the information. The practice of posting accounting records in writing is decreasing as computerized record keeping becomes more widespread. In small businesses, bookkeepers sort and record all the sales slips, bills, check stubs, inventory lists, and requisition lists. They compile figures for cash receipts, accounts payable and receivable, and profits and losses.

Accounting clerks enter and verify transaction data and compute and record various charges. They may also monitor loans and accounts payable and receivable. More advanced clerks may reconcile billing vouchers, while senior workers review invoices and statements.

Accountants set up bookkeeping systems and use bookkeepers' balance sheets to prepare periodic summary statements of financial transactions. Management relies heavily on these bookkeeping records to interpret the organization's overall performance and uses them to make important business decisions. The records are also necessary to file income tax reports and prepare quarterly reports for stockholders.

Bookkeeping and accounting clerks work in retail and wholesale businesses, manufacturing firms, hospitals, schools, charities, and other types of institutional agencies. Many clerks are classified as financial institution bookkeeping and accounting clerks, insurance firm bookkeeping and accounting clerks, hotel bookkeeping and accounting clerks, and railroad bookkeeping and accounting clerks.

General bookkeepers and *general-ledger bookkeepers* are usually employed in smaller business operations. They may perform all the analysis, maintain the financial records, and complete any other tasks that are involved in keeping a full set of bookkeeping records. These employees may have other general office duties, such as mailing statements, answering telephone calls, and filing materials. *Audit clerks* verify figures and may be responsible for sending them on to an *audit clerk supervisor.*

In large companies, an accountant may supervise a department of bookkeepers who perform more specialized work. *Billing and rate clerks* and *fixed capital clerks* may post items in accounts payable or receivable ledgers, make out bills and invoices, or verify the company's rates for certain products and services. *Account information clerks* prepare reports, compile payroll lists and deductions, write company checks, and compute federal tax reports or personnel profit shares. Large companies may employ workers to organize, record, and compute many other types of financial information.

In large business organizations, bookkeepers and accountants may be classified by grades, such as Bookkeeper I or II. The job classification determines their responsibilities.

REQUIREMENTS

High School
In order to be a bookkeeper, you will need at least a high school diploma. It will be helpful to have a background in business mathematics, business writing, typing, and computer training. Pay particular attention to developing sound English and communication skills along with mathematical abilities.

Postsecondary Training
Some employers prefer people who have completed a junior college curriculum or those who have attended a post–high school business training program. In many instances, employers offer on-the-job training for various types of entry-level positions. In some areas, work-study programs are available in which schools, in cooperation with businesses, offer part-time, practical on-the-job training combined with academic study. These programs often help students find immediate employment in similar work after graduation. Local business schools may also offer evening courses.

Certification or Licensing
The American Institute of Professional Bookkeepers offers voluntary certification to bookkeepers who have at least two years of full-time experience (or the part-time or freelance equivalent), pass an examination, and sign a code of ethics. Bookkeepers who complete this requirement may use the designation *certified bookkeeper.*

Employment/Earnings for Bookkeeping and Accounting Clerks by Industry, 2007

Employer	Number Employed	Annual Mean Earnings
Accounting, tax preparation, bookkeeping, and payroll services	93,510	$32,110
Management of companies and enterprises	79,630	$33,750
Local government	75,500	$33,450
Depository credit intermediation	60,050	$30,050
Building equipment contractors	43,430	$34,120
Federal government	18,350	$40,470

Source: U.S. Department of Labor

Other Requirements

Bookkeepers need strong mathematical skills and organizational abilities, and they have to be able to concentrate on detailed work. The work is quite sedentary and often tedious, and you should not mind long hours behind a desk. You should be methodical, accurate, and orderly and enjoy working on detailed tasks. Employers look for honest, discreet, and trustworthy individuals when placing their business in someone else's hands.

Once you are employed as a bookkeeping and accounting clerk, some places of business may require you to have union membership. Larger unions include the Office and Professional Employees International Union; the International Union of Electronic, Electrical, Salaried, Machine, and Furniture Workers-Communications Workers of America; and the American Federation of State, County, and Municipal Employees. Also, depending on the business, clerks may be represented by the same union as other manufacturing employees.

EXPLORING

You can gain experience in bookkeeping by participating in work-study programs or by obtaining part-time or summer work in beginning bookkeeping jobs or related office work. Any retail experience dealing with cash management, pricing, or customer service is also valuable.

You can also volunteer to manage the books for extracurricular student groups. Managing income or cash flow for a club or acting as treasurer for student government are excellent ways to gain experience in maintaining financial records.

Other options are visiting local small businesses to observe their work and talking to representatives of schools that offer business training courses.

EMPLOYERS

Of the approximately 2.1 million bookkeeping, auditing, and accounting clerks, many work for personnel supplying companies; that is, those companies that provide part-time or temporary office workers. Approximately 24 percent of bookkeeping and accounting clerks work part time, according to the U.S. Department of Labor. Many others are employed by government agencies and organizations that provide educational, health, business, and social services.

STARTING OUT

You may find jobs or establish contacts with businesses that are interested in interviewing graduates through your guidance or career services offices. A work-study program or internship may result in a full-time job offer. Business schools and junior colleges generally provide assistance to their graduates in locating employment.

You may locate job opportunities by applying directly to firms or responding to ads online or in newspaper classified sections. State employment agencies and private employment bureaus can also assist in the job search process.

ADVANCEMENT

Bookkeeping workers generally begin their employment by performing routine tasks, such as the simple recording of transactions. Beginners may start as entry-level clerks, cashiers, bookkeeping machine operators, office assistants, or typists. With experience, they may advance to more complex assignments that include computer training in databases and spreadsheets and assume a greater responsibility for the work as a whole.

With experience and education, clerks become department heads or office managers. Further advancement to positions such as office or division manager, department head, accountant, or auditor is possible with a college degree and years of experience. There is a high turnover rate in this field, which increases the promotion opportunities for employees with ability and initiative.

EARNINGS

According to the U.S. Department of Labor, bookkeepers and accounting clerks earned a median income of $31,560 a year in 2007. Earnings are also influenced by such factors as geographic location and the size and type of business for which they are employed. Clerks just starting out earn approximately $20,310 or less. Those with one or two years of college generally earn higher starting wages. Top-paying jobs averaged $47,580 or more a year.

Employees usually receive six to eight paid holidays yearly and one week of paid vacation after six to 12 months of service. Paid vacations may increase to four weeks or more, depending on length of service and place of employment. Fringe benefits may include health and life insurance, sick leave, and retirement plans.

WORK ENVIRONMENT

The majority of office workers, including bookkeeping workers, usually work a 40-hour week, although some employees may work a 35- to 37-hour week. Bookkeeping and accounting clerks usually work in typical office settings. They are more likely to have a cubicle than an office. While the work pace is steady, it can also be routine and repetitive, especially in large companies where the employee is often assigned only one or two specialized job duties.

Attention to numerical details can be physically demanding, and the work can produce eyestrain and nervousness. While bookkeepers usually work with other people and sometimes under close supervision, they can expect to spend most of their day behind a desk; this may seem confining to people who need more variety and stimulation in their work. In addition, the constant attention to detail and the need for accuracy can place considerable responsibility on the worker and cause much stress.

OUTLOOK

A growing number of financial transactions and the implementation of the Sarbanes-Oxley Act of 2002, which requires more accurate reporting of financial data for public companies, has created steady employment growth for bookkeeping and accounting clerks. Employment of bookkeeping and accounting clerks is expected to grow about as fast as the average for all occupations through 2016, according to the U.S. Department of Labor.

There will be numerous replacement job openings, since the turn-over rate in this occupation is high. Offices are centralizing their operations, setting up one center to manage all accounting needs in a single location. As more companies trim back their workforces, opportunities for temporary work should continue to grow.

The automation of office functions will continue to improve over-all worker productivity, which may limit job growth in some settings. Excellent computer skills and professional certification will be vital to securing a job.

FOR MORE INFORMATION

For information on certification and career opportunities, contact
American Institute of Professional Bookkeepers
6001 Montrose Road, Suite 500
Rockville, MD 20852-4873
Tel: 800-622-0121
Email: info@aipb.org
http://www.aipb.org

For information on accredited educational programs, contact
Association to Advance Collegiate Schools of Business
777 South Harbour Island Boulevard, Suite 750
Tampa, FL 33602-5730
Tel: 813-769-6500
http://www.aacsb.edu

For more information on women in accounting, contact
Educational Foundation for Women in Accounting
136 South Keowee Street
Dayton, OH 45402-2241
Tel: 937-424-3391
Email: info@efwa.org
http://www.efwa.org

For free office career and salary information, visit
OfficeTeam
http://www.officeteam.com

Collection Workers

QUICK FACTS

School Subjects
Computer science
Psychology
Speech

Personal Skills
Communication/ideas
Following instructions

Work Environment
Primarily indoors
Primarily one location

Minimum Education Level
High school diploma

Salary Range
$20,630 to $29,990 to
$45,260+

Certification or Licensing
Voluntary

Outlook
Much faster than the average

DOT
241

GOE
09.05.01

NOC
1435

O*NET-SOC
43-3011.00, 43-4041.00,
43-4041.01, 43-4041.02

OVERVIEW

Collection workers—sometimes known as bill collectors, collection correspondents, or collection agents—persuade people to pay their overdue bills. Some work for collection agencies (which are hired by the business to which the money is owed), while others work for department stores, hospitals, banks, public utilities, and other businesses. Collection workers contact delinquent debtors, inform them of the delinquency, and either secure payment or arrange a new payment schedule. If all else fails, they might be forced to repossess property or turn the account over to an attorney for legal proceedings. There are approximately 434,000 collection workers employed in the United States.

HISTORY

Debt collection is one of the world's oldest vocations. In literature, the most famous—and unsuccessful—attempt to retrieve an overdue debt occurred in Shakespeare's Merchant of Venice. Debt collection also figures prominently in the works of Charles Dickens.

In the past, people who were unable to pay their debts suffered great punishments. Some were sent to prison, indentured as servants or slaves until the amount owed was paid off, or recruited by force to colonize new territories. Debtors face less harsh consequences today, but the proliferation of credit opportunities has expanded the field of debt collection. Charge accounts are now offered by department stores, banks, credit unions, oil companies, airlines, and other businesses. Many people buy furniture or other expensive items "on time," meaning they place a small sum down and pay off the balance, plus interest, over a certain period of time. People take out mortgages to finance home purchases and auto loans to finance vehicles. The result of all these credit opportunities is that some people take on too much debt and either fail to meet these obligations or refuse to pay them. When creditors do not receive their payments on time, they employ a collection worker to try and recover the money for them.

THE JOB

A collection worker's main job is to persuade people to pay bills that are past due. The procedure is generally the same in both collection firms and businesses that employ collection workers. The duties of the various workers may overlap, depending on the size and nature of the company.

When routine billing methods—monthly statements and notice letters—fail to secure payment, the collection worker receives a bad-debt file (usually an electronic file downloaded to the agency's computer system). This file contains information about the debtor, the nature and amount of the unpaid bill, the last charge incurred, and the date of the last payment. The collection worker then contacts the debtor by phone or mail to request full or partial payment or, if necessary, to arrange a new payment schedule.

Terrence Sheffert is a collection worker for a collection agency based in Chicago. He describes his typical duties as making phone calls and writing letters. "I am usually in the office, on the phone with clients or the people who owe them," he says. "I never actually go out to make collections, but there are some agents who do."

If the bill has not been paid because the customer believes it is incorrect, the merchandise purchased was faulty, or the service billed for was not performed, the collector takes appropriate steps to settle the matter. If, after investigation, the debt collector finds that the debt is still valid, he or she again tries to secure payment.

In cases where the customer has not paid because of a financial emergency or poor money management, the debt collector may arrange a new payment schedule. In instances where the customer goes to great or fraudulent lengths to avoid payment, the collector may recommend that the file be turned over to an attorney. "Every day, we are protecting the clients' interests and getting the money," Sheffert says. "If we can't get it, then we'll call in legal representation to handle it."

When all efforts to obtain payment fail, a collection worker known as a *repossessor* may be assigned to find the merchandise on which the debtor still owes money and return it to the seller. Such goods as furniture or appliances can be picked up in a truck.

To reclaim automobiles and other motor vehicles, the repossessor might be forced to enter and start the vehicle with special tools if the buyer does not surrender the key.

In large agencies, some collection workers specialize as *skip tracers*. Skip tracers are assigned to find debtors who "skip" out on their debts—that is, who move without notifying their creditors so that they don't have to pay their bills. Skip tracers act like detectives, searching telephone directories and street listings and making inquiries at post offices in an effort to locate missing debtors. Increasingly such information can be found through online computer databases (some agencies subscribe to a service to collect this information). Skip tracers also try to find a person's whereabouts by contacting former neighbors and employers, local merchants, friends, relatives, and references listed on the original credit application. They follow every lead and prepare a report of the entire investigation.

In some small offices, collection workers perform clerical duties, such as reading and answering correspondence, filing, or posting amounts paid to people's accounts. They might offer financial advice to customers or contact them to inquire about their satisfaction with the handling of the account. In larger companies, *credit and loan collection supervisors* might oversee the activities of several other collection workers.

REQUIREMENTS

High School

Most employers prefer to hire high school graduates for collection jobs, but formal education beyond high school is typically not required. High school courses that might prove helpful in this career include those that will help you communicate clearly and properly, such as English and speech. Because collection workers have to talk with people about a very delicate subject, psychology classes might also be beneficial. Finally, computer classes are good choices, since this career, like most others, often requires at least some familiarity with keyboarding, basic computer operation, and Internet research strategies.

Postsecondary Training

Most collection workers learn collection procedures and telephone techniques on the job in a training period spent under the guidance of a supervisor or an experienced collector. The legal restrictions on collection activities, such as when and how calls can be made, are also covered.

ACA International conducts a variety of seminars on collection techniques, state and federal compliance laws that pertain to collection workers, and other topics.

Certification or Licensing

Although it is not required by law, some employers require their employees to become certified by the Association of Credit and Collection Professionals, which offers several certifications, including professional collection specialist, creditor collection specialist, health care collection specialist, and higher education collection specialist. To learn more, visit http://www.acainternational.org. The National Association of Credit Management also offers certification to credit industry professionals.

Other Requirements

Because this is a people-oriented job, you must have a pleasant manner and voice. You may spend much of your time on the telephone speaking with people about overdue payments, which can be a delicate subject. To succeed as a collector, you must be sympathetic and tactful, yet assertive and persuasive enough to convince debtors to pay their overdue bills. In addition, collectors must be alert, quick-witted, and imaginative to handle the unpredictable and potentially awkward situations in this type of work.

Collection work can be emotionally taxing. It involves listening to a bill payer's problems and occasional verbal attacks directed at both the collector and the company. Some people physically threaten repossessors and other collection workers. "The best description of this job would be stressful," Terrence Sheffert says. "Everything about collecting is very stressful." In the face of these stresses, you must be able to avoid becoming upset, personally involved with, or alarmed by angry or threatening debtors. This requires a cool head and an even temperament.

EXPLORING

The best way to explore collection work is to secure part-time or summer employment in a collection agency or credit office. You might also find it helpful to interview a collection worker to obtain firsthand information about the practical aspects of this occupation. Finally, the associations listed at the end of this article may be able to provide further information about the career.

EMPLOYERS

Of the approximately 434,000 collection workers in the United States, about 24 percent work for collection agencies. Collection agencies are usually independent companies that are hired by various businesses to collect debt that is owed them. Other bill collectors

Facts About Collections

- Third-party debt collectors returned $40.4 billion in debt to creditors in 2007. This is the equivalent of an average savings of $354 per U.S. household "that might have otherwise been spent had businesses been forced to raise prices to cover the unrecovered debt," according to a survey by PricewaterhouseCoopers.
- There are about 6,500 collection agencies in the United States.
- Approximately 67 percent of collection workers are women.

Sources: ACA International, ACA International, MarketData Enterprises

work for a wide range of organizations and businesses that extend credit to customers. Department stores, hospitals, banks, public utilities, and auto financing companies are examples of businesses that frequently hire bill collectors.

The companies that hire collection workers are located throughout the United States, especially in heavily populated urban areas. Companies that have branch offices in rural communities often locate their collection departments in nearby cities.

STARTING OUT

Terrence Sheffert got started in collection work because it was a family profession. "My whole family is in collecting, so I thought, 'Hey, I'll go for it,'" he says. If you are interested in becoming a collection worker, one easy way to start a job search is to apply directly to collection agencies, credit reporting companies, banks, and major retailers that sell large items. To find collection agencies and credit reporting companies, try doing a simple online search. Another easy way is to look in your local yellow pages—or expand your search by going to the library and looking through yellow pages of other cities. Remember that these sorts of jobs are often more plentiful in more urban areas.

You should also check the classified ads of area newspapers for headings such as "Billing" or "Collection." Finally, job openings may be listed at your local employment office.

ADVANCEMENT

Experienced collection workers who have displayed above-average ability can advance to management positions, such as supervisors or *collection managers.* These workers generally have responsibility for the operations of a specific shift, location, or department of a collection company. They oversee other collection workers. Other avenues of advancement might include becoming a *credit authorizer, credit checker,* or *bank loan officer.* Credit authorizers approve questionable charges against customers' existing accounts by evaluating the customers' computerized credit records and payment histories. Credit checkers in credit bureaus—sometimes also called *credit investigators* or *credit reporters*—search for, update, and verify information for credit reports. Loan officers help borrowers fill out loan applications, verify and analyze applications, and decide whether and how much to loan applicants. Some experienced and successful collection workers might open their own agencies. This is Terrence Sheffert's goal. "I hope to advance from collection to management, and then open up my own business," he says.

EARNINGS

Collection workers might receive a salary plus a bonus or commission on the debt amounts they collect. Others work for a flat salary with no commissions. Since the pay system varies among different companies, incomes vary substantially. In 2007 the median hourly wage for bill collectors working full time was $14.42, according to the U.S. Department of Labor. This hourly wage translates into a yearly income of approximately $29,990. Earnings for collection workers ranged from less than $20,630 to more than $45,260 annually.

Depending on their employer, some full-time bill collectors receive a benefits package that may include paid holidays and vacations, sick leave, and health and dental insurance.

WORK ENVIRONMENT

Most collectors work in pleasant offices, sit at a desk, and spend a great deal of time on the telephone. Because they spend so much time on the phone, many collectors use phone headsets and program-operated dialing systems. Because most companies use computers to store information about their accounts, the collection worker frequently works on a computer. He or she may sit in front of a computer monitor, reviewing and entering information about the account while talking to the debtor on the phone.

Rarely does a collector have to make a personal visit to a customer. Repossession proceedings are undertaken only in extreme cases.

Terrence Sheffert works a 40-hour week, from 9:00 A.M. to 5:00 P.M., Monday through Friday. Some collection workers stagger their schedules, however. They might start late in the morning and work into the evening, or they might take a weekday off and work on Saturday. Evening and weekend work is common, because debtors are often home during these times.

OUTLOOK

The U.S. Department of Labor predicts that employment of collection workers will grow much faster than the average for all careers through 2016. This demand is due in part to the relaxed standards for credit cards, which means more people, regardless of their financial circumstances, are able to get credit cards, make purchases on credit, and build up large debts they have difficulty repaying. The U.S. Department of Labor also notes that hospitals and physicians' offices are two of the fastest growing employers of bill collectors and collection agencies. This is largely because health insurance plans frequently do not adequately cover payment for medical procedures, and patients are often left with large bills that they have difficulty repaying. Economic recessions also increase the amount of personal debt that goes unpaid. Therefore, unlike many occupations, collection workers usually find that their employment and workloads increase during economic slumps. Government agencies—including the Internal Revenue Service—are also expected to employ more collection workers in the future.

FOR MORE INFORMATION

For a brochure on careers in collection work and information on certification, contact
ACA International
PO Box 390106
Minneapolis, MN 55439-0106
Tel: 952-926-6547
Email: aca@acainternational.org
http://www.acainternational.org

For information on careers and certification, contact
National Association of Credit Management
8840 Columbia 100 Parkway
Columbia, MD 21045-2158
Tel: 410-740-5560
http://www.nacm.org

Counter and Retail Clerks

OVERVIEW

Counter and retail clerks work as intermediaries between the general public and businesses that provide goods and services. They take orders and receive payments for such services as DVD rentals, automobile rentals, and laundry and dry cleaning. They often assist customers with their purchasing or rental decisions, especially when sales personnel are not available. These workers might also prepare billing statements, keep records of receipts and sales, and balance money in their cash registers. There are approximately 477,000 counter and retail clerks working in the United States.

HISTORY

The first retail outlets in the United States sold food staples, farm necessities, and clothing. Many of these businesses also served as the post office and became the social and economic centers of their communities. Owners of these general stores often performed all the jobs in the business.

Over the years retailing has undergone numerous changes. Large retail stores, requiring many workers, including counter and retail clerks, became more common. Also emerging were specialized retail or chain outlets—clothing stores, bicycle shops, computer shops, video stores, and athletic footwear boutiques—which also needed counter and retail clerks to assist customers and to receive payment for services or products.

THE JOB

Job duties vary depending on the type of business. In a shoe repair shop, for example, the clerk receives the shoes to be repaired or cleaned from the customer, examines the shoes, gives a price quote and a receipt to the customer, and then sends the shoes to the work department for the necessary repairs or cleaning. The shoes are marked with a tag specifying what work needs to be done and to whom the shoes belong. After the work is completed, the clerk returns the shoes to the customer and collects payment.

In stores where customers rent equipment or merchandise, clerks prepare rental forms and quote rates to customers. The clerks answer customer questions about the operation of the equipment. They often take a deposit to cover any accidents or possible damage. Clerks also check the equipment to be certain it is in good working order and make minor adjustments, if necessary. With long-term rentals, such as storage-facility rentals, clerks notify the customers when the rental period is about to expire and when the rent is overdue. *Video-rental clerks* greet customers, check out DVDs or tapes, and accept payment. Upon return of the DVDs or tapes, the clerks check the condition of the DVDs or tapes and then put them back on the shelves.

In smaller shops with no sales personnel or in situations when the sales personnel are unavailable, counter and retail clerks assist customers with purchases or rentals by demonstrating the merchandise, answering customers' questions, accepting payment, recording sales, and wrapping the purchases or arranging for their delivery.

In addition to these duties, clerks sometimes prepare billing statements to be sent to customers. They might keep records of receipts and sales throughout the day and balance the money in their registers when their work shift ends. They sometimes are responsible for the display and presentation of products in their store. In supermarkets and grocery stores, clerks stock shelves and bag food purchases for the customers.

Service-establishment attendants work in various types of businesses, such as a laundry, where attendants take clothes to be cleaned or repaired and write down the customer's name and address. *Watch-and-clock-repair clerks* receive clocks and watches for repair and examine the timepieces to estimate repair costs. They might make minor repairs, such as replacing a watchband; otherwise, the timepiece is forwarded to the repair shop with a description of needed repairs.

Many clerks have job titles that describe what they do and where they work. These include *laundry-pricing clerks, photo-processing counter clerks, tool-and-equipment-rental clerks, airplane-charter clerks, baby-stroller and wheelchair-rental clerks,*

Rental car agents assist customers. (*Jeff Greenberg/The Image Works*)

storage-facility-rental clerks, boat-rental clerks, trailer-rental clerks, automobile-rental clerks, fur-storage clerks, and *self-service-laundry and dry-cleaning attendants.*

REQUIREMENTS

High School

High school courses useful for the job include English, speech, and mathematics, as well as any business-related classes, such as typing, computer science, and those covering principles of retailing. Although there are no specific educational requirements for clerk positions, most employers prefer to hire high school graduates. Legible handwriting and the ability to add and subtract numbers quickly are also necessary.

Certification or Licensing

The National Retail Federation offers the following voluntary certifications for counter and retail clerks: national professional certification in customer service, national professional certification in sales, and basics of retail credential. Contact the federation for more information.

Other Requirements

To be a counter and retail clerk, you should have a pleasant personality and an ability to interact with a variety of people. You should also be neat and well groomed and have a high degree of personal responsibility. Counter and retail clerks must be able to adjust to alternating periods of heavy and light activity. No two days—or even customers—are alike. Because some customers can be rude or even hostile, you must exercise tact and patience at all times.

EXPLORING

There are numerous opportunities for part-time or temporary work as a clerk, especially during the holiday season. Many high schools have developed work-study programs that combine courses in retailing with part-time work in the field. Store owners cooperating in these programs may hire you as a full-time worker after you complete the course.

EMPLOYERS

Of the numerous types of clerks working in the United States, approximately 477,000 work as counter and rental clerks at video rental stores, dry cleaners, car rental agencies, and other such establishments. These are not the only employers of clerks, however; hardware stores, shoe stores, moving businesses, camera stores—in fact, nearly any business that sells goods or provides services to the general public employs clerks. Many work on a part-time basis.

STARTING OUT

If you are interested in securing an entry-level position as a clerk, you should contact stores directly. Workers with some experience, such as those who have completed a work-study program in high school, should have the greatest success, but most entry-level positions do not require any previous experience. Jobs are often listed in help-wanted advertisements.

Most stores provide new workers with on-the-job training in which experienced clerks explain company policies and procedures and teach new employees how to operate the cash register and other equipment. This training usually continues for several weeks until the new employee feels comfortable on the job.

ADVANCEMENT

Counter and retail clerks usually begin their employment doing routine tasks, such as checking stock and operating the cash register. With experience, they might advance to more complicated assignments and assume some sales responsibilities. Those with the skill and aptitude might become salespeople or store managers, although further education is normally required for management positions.

The high turnover rate in the clerk position increases the opportunities for being promoted. The number and kind of opportunities, however, depend on the place of employment and the ability, training, and experience of the employee.

EARNINGS

According to the U.S. Department of Labor, the median hourly wage for counter and retail clerks was $9.65 in 2007. Working year round at 40 hours per week, a clerk earning this wage would make approximately $20,070 annually. Ten percent of counter and retail clerks earned less than $6.92 per hour (approximately $14,400 annually) in 2007, and 10 percent earned more than $18.57 per hour (or $38,620 annually). Wages among clerks vary for a number of reasons, including the industry in which they work. The U.S. Department of Labor reports, for example, that those working in the automobile equipment rental and leasing field had mean hourly earnings of $11.90 (approximately $24,740 per year) in 2007, while those in dry cleaning and laundry services earned a mean of $8.79 per hour (approximately $18,280 yearly). Wages also vary among clerks due to factors such as size of the business, location in the country, and experience of the employee.

Those workers who have union affiliation (usually those who work for supermarkets) may earn considerably more than their nonunion counterparts. Full-time workers, especially those who are union members, might also receive benefits such as paid vacation time and health insurance, but this is not the industry norm. Some businesses offer merchandise discounts for their employees. Part-time workers usually receive fewer benefits than those working full time.

WORK ENVIRONMENT

Although a 40-hour workweek is common, many stores operate on a 44- to 48-hour workweek. Most stores are open on Saturday and many on Sunday. Most stores are also open one or more weekday evenings, so a clerk's working hours might vary from week to week and include evening and weekend shifts. Many counter and retail clerks work overtime during Christmas and other rush seasons. Part-time clerks generally work during peak business periods.

Most clerks work indoors in well-ventilated and well-lighted environments. The job can be routine and repetitive, and clerks often spend much of their time on their feet.

OUTLOOK

The U.S. Department of Labor predicts that employment for counter and retail clerks will grow much faster than the average for all occupations through 2016. Businesses that focus on customer service will always want to hire friendly and responsible clerks. Major employers should be those providing rental products and services. Because of the high turnover in this field, however, many job openings will come from the need to replace workers. Opportunities for temporary or part-time work should be good, especially during busy business periods. Employment opportunities for clerks are plentiful in large metropolitan areas, where their services are in great demand.

FOR MORE INFORMATION

For information about careers in the retail industry and certification, contact
National Retail Federation
325 7th Street, NW, Suite 1100
Washington, DC 20004-2818
Tel: 800-673-4692
http://www.nrf.com

For information on scholarships and internships, contact
Retail Industry Leaders Association
1700 North Moore Street, Suite 2250
Arlington, VA 22209-1933
Tel: 703-841-2300
http://www.rila.org

Financial Institution Tellers, Clerks, and Related Workers

OVERVIEW

Financial institution tellers, clerks, and related workers perform many tasks in banks and other savings institutions. Tellers work at teller windows where they receive and pay out money, record customer transactions, cash checks, sell traveler's checks, and perform other banking duties. The most familiar teller is the *commercial teller*, who cashes checks and processes deposits and withdrawals. Specialized tellers often work at large financial institutions. Clerks' and related workers' jobs usually vary with the size of the institution. In small banks, a clerk or related worker may perform a combination of tasks, while in larger banks an employee may be assigned to one specialized duty. All banking activities are concerned with the safekeeping, exchange, record keeping, and credit use of money. There are approximately 608,000 tellers employed in the United States.

HISTORY

The profession of banking is nearly as old as civilization itself. Ancient records show that the Babylonians, for example, had a fairly complex system of lending, borrowing, and depositing money even before 2500 B.C. Other early literature makes reference to "money-lenders" and "money-changers" as ancient writers and travelers described how they

QUICK FACTS

School Subjects
Business
Computer science
Mathematics

Personal Skills
Following instructions
Mechanical/manipulative

Work Environment
Primarily indoors
Primarily one location

Minimum Education Level
Some postsecondary training

Salary Range
$17,360 to $25,000 to
  $47,580+

Certification or Licensing
None available

Outlook
About as fast as the average
  (tellers)
More slowly than the average
  (clerks and related workers)

DOT
211, 216

GOE
09.05.01

NOC
1434

O*NET-SOC
43-3021.01, 43-3031.00,
  43-3071.00, 43-5021.00

bought money in other countries by trading coins from their own homelands.

The term *bank* is derived from the Italian *banco,* meaning bench. Since the time of the Roman Empire, Italy has been an important trading and shipping nation. In medieval times, bankers set up benches on the streets and from these conducted their business of trading currencies and accepting precious metals and jewels for safekeeping. They also lent money at interest to finance the new ventures of shipping merchants and other businesses. Italian cities eventually established permanent banks, and this practice gradually spread north throughout Europe. During the 17th century important banking developments took place in England, which by that time had become a major trading nation. In 1694 the Bank of England was founded in London.

In the United States the Continental Congress chartered the Bank of North America in 1782 in Philadelphia. The first state bank was chartered in Boston in 1784 as the Bank of Massachusetts. Although the development of banking in the United States has experienced periods of slow growth and numerous failures throughout history, Congress and the federal government have done a great deal to make the nation's banking system safer and more effective.

Today, banking, like many other professions, has turned to the use of automation, mechanization, computers, telecommunications, and many modern methods of bookkeeping and record systems. Banks and savings institutions employ thousands of workers so that they can offer all the modern banking conveniences that Americans enjoy today.

THE JOB

Several different types of tellers may work at a financial institution, depending on its size. The teller the average bank customer has the most contact with is the commercial teller, also known as a *paying and receiving teller*. These tellers service the public directly by accepting customers' deposits and providing them with receipts, paying out withdrawals and recording the transactions, cashing checks, exchanging money for customers to provide them with certain kinds of change or currency, and accepting deposits. At the beginning of the workday, each teller is given a cash drawer from the vault containing a certain amount of cash. During the day this is the money they use for transactions with customers. Their work with the money and their record keeping must be accurate. At the end of their shifts, the tellers' cash drawers are recounted, and the amount must match up with the transactions done that day. A teller who has problems balancing his or her drawer won't be employed for very long.

Head tellers and *teller supervisors* train tellers, arrange work schedules, and monitor the tellers' records of the day's transactions. If there are any problems in balancing the cash drawers, the head teller or supervisor must try to figure out where the error occurred and reconcile the differences.

At large financial institutions, tellers may perform specialized duties and are identified by the transactions they handle. *Note tellers*, for example, are responsible for receiving and issuing receipts or payments on promissory notes and recording these transactions correctly. *Discount tellers* are responsible for issuing and collecting customers' notes. *Foreign banknote tellers* work in the exchange department, where they buy and sell foreign currency. When customers need to trade their foreign currency for U.S. currency, these tellers determine the current value of the foreign currency in dollars, count out the bills requested by the customer, and make change. These tellers may also sell foreign currency and traveler's checks for people traveling out of the country. *Collection and exchange tellers* accept payments in forms other than cash—contracts, mortgages, and bonds, for example.

While tellers' work involves much interaction with the public, most of the work done by clerks and other related workers is completed behind the scenes. Clerks and related workers are responsible for keeping depositors' money safe, the bank's investments healthy, and government regulations satisfied. All such workers assist in processing the vast amounts of paperwork that a bank generates. This paperwork may consist of deposit slips, checks, financial statements to customers, correspondence, record transactions, and reports for internal and external use. Depending on their job responsibilities, clerks may prepare, collect, send, index, or file these documents. In addition, they may talk with customers and other banks, take telephone calls, respond to emails, and perform other general office duties.

The tasks clerks and related workers perform also depend on the size of the financial institution. Duties may be more generalized in smaller facilities and very specialized at larger institutions. The nature of the bank's business and the array of services it offers may also determine a clerk's duties. Services may differ somewhat in a commercial bank from those in a savings bank, trust company, credit union, or savings and loan. In the past, banks generally lent money to businesses, while savings and loan and credit unions lent to individuals, but these differences are slowly disappearing over time.

Collection clerks process checks, coupons, and drafts that customers present to the financial institution for special handling. *Commodity-loan clerks* keep track of commodities (usually farm products) used as collateral by the foreign departments of large banks.

Banks employ *bookkeepers* to keep track of countless types of financial and administrative information. *Bookkeeping clerks* file checks, alphabetize paperwork to assist senior bookkeepers, and sort and list various other kinds of material.

Proof machine operators handle a machine that, in one single operation, can sort checks and other papers, add their amounts, and record totals. *Transit clerks* sort and list checks and drafts on other banks and prepare them for mailing or electronic transmission to those banks. *Statement clerks* send customers their account statements listing the withdrawals and deposits they have made.

Messengers deliver checks, drafts, letters, and other business papers to other financial institutions, business firms, and local and federal government agencies. Messengers who work only within the bank are often known as *pages*. *Trust-mail clerks* keep track of mail in trust departments.

Other clerks—*collateral-and-safekeeping clerks*, *reserves clerks*, and *interest clerks*—collect and record information about collateral, reserves, and interest rates and payments. *Letter-of-credit clerks* keep track of letters of credit for export and import purposes. *Wire-transfer clerks* operate machines that direct the transfer of funds from one account to another.

Many banks now use computers to perform the routine tasks that workers formerly did by hand. *Encoder operators* run machines that print information on checks and other papers in magnetic ink so that machines can read them. *Control clerks* keep track of all the data and paperwork transacted through the electronic data processing divisions.

In addition to working in banks, people employed by financial institutions may work at savings and loan associations, personal finance companies, credit unions, government agencies, and large businesses operating credit offices. Although tellers, clerks, and other workers' duties may differ among institutions, the needs for accuracy and honesty are the same. Financial institutions are usually pleasant, quiet places to work and have very up-to-date equipment and business machines. People who work in banking should be of good character and enjoy detailed work.

REQUIREMENTS
High School
Most banks today prefer to hire individuals who have completed high school. If you take courses in bookkeeping, mathematics, business arithmetic, and business machines while in high school, you may have an advantage when applying for a job. In addition, anyone

working in a bank should be able to use computers, so be sure to take computer science courses. Take English, speech, and foreign language classes to improve your communication skills, which you will need when interacting with customers and other workers. Some banks are interested in hiring college graduates (or those who have completed at least two years of college training) who can eventually move into managerial positions. Exchange clerks may be expected to know foreign languages.

Postsecondary Training

Once hired, tellers, clerks, and related workers typically receive on-the-job training. At large institutions, tellers usually receive about one week of classroom training and then undergo on-the-job training for several weeks before they are allowed to work independently. Smaller financial institutions may only provide the on-the-job training in which experienced employees supervise new tellers. Clerks may also need to undergo classroom instruction; for example, a bookkeeping clerk may need to take a class covering a certain computer program.

To enhance your chances of getting a job and hone your skills, you may want to take business-related courses or courses for those in the financial industry at a local community college. Courses that may be helpful to take include records management, office systems and procedures, and computer database programming. Those with the most skills and training will find they usually have the best possibilities for advancing.

Numerous educational opportunities will be available to you once you have begun working—and gaining experience—in the financial world. For example, the American Institute of Banking (the educational division of the American Bankers Association) has a vast array of adult education classes in business fields and offers training courses in numerous parts of the country that enable people to earn standard or graduate certificates in bank training. Individuals may also enroll in correspondence study courses.

Other Requirements

Because the work involves many details, a prime requirement for all bank employees is accuracy. Even the slightest error can cause untold extra hours of work and inconvenience or even monetary loss. A pleasing and congenial personality and the ability to get along well with fellow workers and the public are also necessary in this employment.

The physical requirements of the work are not very demanding, although many of these workers spend much of the day standing, which can be tiring. While working in this field, you will be expected to be neat, clean, and appropriately dressed for business.

Banks occasionally require lie detector tests of applicants, as well as fingerprint and background investigations if the job requires handling currency and finances. Those employees handling money or having access to confidential financial information may have to qualify for a personal bond. Some banks now require pre-employment drug testing, and random testing for drugs while under employment is becoming common practice.

Although integrity and honesty are important traits for an employee in any type of work, they are absolutely necessary if you hope to be employed in banks and other financial institutions where large sums of money are handled every day. Workers must exhibit sound judgment and intelligence.

EXPLORING

You can explore the jobs in this field by visiting local financial institutions and talking with the directors of personnel or with people who work in these jobs. You should also consider serving as treasurer for your student government or a club that you are interested in. This will give you experience working with numbers and handling finances, as well as the opportunity to demonstrate responsibility. Learn about finances and the different kinds of financial instruments available by reading publications such as the business section of your local paper and *Money* magazine (also online at http://money.cnn.com).

Sometimes banks offer part-time employment to young people who feel they have a definite interest in pursuing a career in banking or those with business and clerical skills. Other types of part-time employment—where you learn basic business skills, how to interact with the public, and how to work well with other employees—may also be valuable training for those planning to enter these occupations.

EMPLOYERS

Approximately 608,000 tellers are employed in the United States—with about 25 percent working part time. Financial institution tellers, clerks, and related workers are employed by commercial banks and other depository institutions and by mortgage banks and other nondepository institutions.

STARTING OUT

Private and state employment agencies frequently list available positions for financial institution tellers, clerks, and related workers. Newspaper help-wanted advertisements carry listings for such employees. Some large financial institutions visit schools and colleges to recruit qualified applicants to fill positions on their staff.

If you are interested in a job as a financial institution teller or clerk, try contacting the human resources director at a bank or other institution to see if any positions are available. If any jobs are open, you may be asked to come in and fill out an application. It is very important, however, to arrange the appointment first by telephone or mail because drop-in visits are disruptive and seldom welcome.

If you know someone who is willing to give you a personal introduction to the human resources director or to the officers of a bank, you may find that this will help you secure employment. Personal and business references can be important to bank employers when they hire new personnel.

Many financial institution clerks begin their employment as trainees in certain types of work, such as business machine operation or general or specialized clerical duties. Employees may start out as file clerks, transit clerks, or bookkeeping clerks and in some cases as pages or messengers. In general, beginning jobs are determined by the size of the institution and the nature of its operations. In banking work, employees are sometimes trained in related job tasks so that they might be promoted later.

ADVANCEMENT

Many banks and financial institutions follow a "promote-from-within" policy. Promotions are usually given on the basis of past job performance and consider the employee's seniority, ability, and general personal qualities. Clerks who have done well and established good reputations may be promoted to teller positions. Tellers, in turn, may be promoted to head teller or supervisory positions such as department head. Some head tellers may be transferred from their main branch bank to a smaller branch bank where they have greater responsibilities.

Employees who show initiative in their jobs and pursue additional education may advance into low-level officer positions, such as assistant trust officer. The Bank Administration Institute and the American Institute of Banking (a division of the American Bankers Association) offer courses in various banking topics that can help employees learn new skills and prepare for promotions.

Advancement into the highest level positions typically require the employee to earn a college or advanced degree.

EARNINGS

The earnings of financial institution workers vary by their specific duties, size and type of institution, and area of the country. According to the U.S. Department of Labor, full-time tellers earned a median annual income of about $22,920 in 2007. Salaries ranged from less than $17,360 to more than $31,200.

The U.S. Department of Labor also reports that bookkeeping, accounting, and auditing clerks earned a median full-time salary of $31,560 in 2007. The lowest paid 10 percent earned less than $20,310, and the highest paid 10 percent earned more than $47,580 a year. General office clerks employed in banks had medial annual earnings of $24,586 in 2006.

Financial institution tellers, clerks, and related workers may receive up to 12 paid holidays a year, depending on their locale. A two-week paid vacation is common after one year of service and can increase to three weeks after 10 or 15 years of service. Fringe benefits usually include group life and health insurance, hospitalization, and jointly financed retirement plans.

WORK ENVIRONMENT

Most financial institution workers work a 40-hour week. Tellers may need to work irregular hours or overtime, since many banks stay open until 8:00 P.M. on Fridays and are open Saturday mornings to accommodate their customers. Bank clerks and accounting department employees may have to work overtime at least once a week and often at the close of each month's banking operations to process important paperwork. Check-processing workers who are employed in large financial institutions may work late evening or night shifts. Those employees engaged in computer operations may also work evening or night shifts because this equipment is usually run around the clock. Pay for overtime work is usually straight compensation.

Banks and other depository institutions are usually air-conditioned, pleasantly decorated, and comfortably furnished. Financial institutions have excellent alarm systems and many built-in features that offer protection to workers and facilities. Although the work is not physically strenuous, tellers do have to spend much of their time on their feet. The work clerks and others perform is usually of a very repetitive nature, and the duties are very similar from day to day. Most of the work is paperwork, computer entry, data processing, and other mechanical processes. Clerks do not frequently have contact with customers or clients. Tellers, on the other hand, have extended contact with the public and must always remain polite, even under trying circumstances. Tellers, clerks, and others must be able to work closely with each other, sometimes on joint tasks, as well as under supervision.

OUTLOOK

The U.S. Department of Labor predicts that employment for financial institution tellers will grow about as fast as the average for all careers through 2016. Until recently, there was a projected decline caused by overexpansion by banks and competition from companies offering bank-like services, and the prevalence of automated banking technologies. However, the increased numbers of bank branches, together with longer hours and more services offered to draw in more customers, will require more tellers. Prospects are best for tellers who have excellent customer skills and are knowledgeable about financial services.

The increasing use of automatic teller machines, banking by telephone and computer, and other technologies has increased teller efficiency—which will eventually cause a reduced need for tellers. Many employment opportunities for tellers will come from the need to replace those who have left the field.

Employment outlook for clerks and related workers is expected to grow more slowly than the average for all occupations through 2016. Mergers and the use of computers and automated technologies contribute to containing the number of new positions available. Due to the repetitive nature of this work, turnover is high. Most job openings come from the need to find replacement workers for those who have left. In addition, financial institutions need to employ a large number of people to function properly.

The increasing use of computers and electronic data processing methods will continue to curtail the numbers of workers needed for these positions. Nevertheless, because of the large size of these occupations, there should be many opportunities for replacement workers.

FOR MORE INFORMATION

The ABA has general information about the banking industry and information on education available through the American Institute of Banking.
American Bankers Association (ABA)
1120 Connecticut Avenue, NW
Washington, DC 20036-3902

Tel: 800-226-5377
http://www.aba.com

BAI offers online courses such as "Introduction to Checks" and "Cash Handling Techniques." For more information, visit its Web site.
Bank Administration Institue (BAI)
115 South LaSalle Street, Suite 3300
Chicago, IL 60603-3801
Tel: 888-284-4078
Email: info@bai.org
http://www.bai.org

INTERVIEW

Lucinda Rietcheck is a teller at Legacy Bank in Wichita, Kansas. She discussed her career with the editors of Careers in Focus: Clerks and Administrative Workers.

Q. How long have you worked in the field?

A. I have been a teller for the last three years and eight months, and of that, I have worked at Legacy Bank a year and a half.

Q. How and where did you get your first job in this field?

A. One day, I went into my local branch of Intrust Bank (here in Wichita, Kansas). One of the tellers there asked if I was looking for a job. At the time, I was receiving very few hours with my current employer. Shortly thereafter, I applied for the part-time teller job they had available for that branch. I was hired, and soon discovered how much I enjoyed being a teller.

Q. What do you like most and least about your job?

A. I absolutely love that I get to interact with people as a teller. However, there are moments when I have a difficult time with having the patience for customers' complaints, but this does have an "up-side." One can learn from those situations and use them to address similar future problems. I always say that customer complaints are a great learning source. All banks can benefit from customer complaints because they're not only a great way to teach employees about how to solve problems, but the bank can also learn how to better itself by this.

Q. What is your work environment like?

A. The branch I work at is an easy-going location. Everyone generally gets along with one another, and we strive to work our hardest at every task we do. Most of all, I love how we make a great team!

Q. What advice would you give to high school students who are interested in this career?

A. I would tell them that while it's an enjoyable career, it's definitely one you need to take very seriously. It can be a stressful job at times, but that is to be expected with any job. Also, make sure you research the career field you're going into so there are no surprises. A great way to do this is by talking to people you know who have those jobs themselves.

Q. What are the most important professional qualities for bank tellers?

A. I believe that all tellers must be dressed professionally no matter what the bank requires for their dress code. Both men and women need to make sure their hair is not in disarray. Their clothes should be appropriate for the position and properly pressed.

Hotel Desk Clerks

QUICK FACTS

School Subjects
Business
Computer science
Speech

Personal Skills
Following instructions
Helping/teaching

Work Environment
Primarily indoors
Primarily one location

Minimum Education Level
High school diploma

Salary Range
$14,480 to $18,950 to
$27,890+

Certification or Licensing
Voluntary

Outlook
Faster than the average

DOT
238

GOE
09.05.01

NOC
6435

O*NET-SOC
43-4081.00

OVERVIEW

Hotel desk clerks work the front desk and are responsible for performing a variety of services, such as registering guests, assigning rooms, and providing general information. For many guests, the front desk worker gives them their first impression of the hotel. There are about 219,000 desk clerks employed at lodging properties, large and small, in the United States.

HISTORY

The very first desk clerks were simply the owners of a lodging establishment or members of their family. Besides managing the inn, cleaning the rooms, and cooking the food, the innkeepers were responsible for assigning rooms and collecting fees. As hotels grew bigger, many consolidated to create chains, such as the Statler Hotels or Holiday Inn. Sometimes a single owner was responsible for a number of properties. Innkeepers realized they needed help from employees apart from their immediate families. Desk clerks were trusted with managing the duties of the front desk—welcoming guests, assigning rooms, and maintaining hotel records.

Today, front office workers rely on computers to reduce paperwork, keep better records, and manage reservation systems. New software is constantly being developed to help the front office. For example, many guests now opt to use the in-room video express checkout instead of waiting in line. Even with such technological advancements, desk clerks are still needed to staff the front desk. Guests like personal attention to certain details such as answering their questions

Two hotel desk clerks review guest reservations. (*Jeff Greenberg/ The Image Works*)

and handling special requests. Even video checkouts are processed by desk clerks, who also then mail folios to guests.

THE JOB

The duties of the desk clerk, also known as *front office worker*, can be separated into four categories: process reservations, register the guest, serve as primary guest liaison, and process guest departure.

Process reservations. Desk clerks, or more specifically, *reservation clerks*, handle the duties of guest reservations, most often over the phone. They determine if the requested date is available, quote rates, record advance deposits or prepayments, confirm room reservations, and describe policies and services to guests. When dealing with reservation discrepancies, reservation clerks may have to retrieve hotel records or change or cancel the reservation to resolve the problem to the guest's satisfaction. Reservation clerks must also analyze the guest's special needs while at the hotel and relay them to the proper department.

Register the guest. After greeting the guest, desk clerks obtain and verify the required registration information, such as the guest's name, address, and length of stay. A credit card is usually required

Facts About the U.S. Lodging Industry, 2007

- There were 48,062 lodging properties with 15 or more rooms.
- A total of 4,476,191 rooms were available at these properties.
- The average occupancy rate was 63.1 percent.
- The average room rate was $103.87 in 2007—up from $83.54 in 2002.
- The travel and tourism industry (which includes lodging properties, restaurants, airlines, car rental agencies, cruise lines, travel agents, and tour operators) ranks among the top 10 industries in 49 states and the District of Columbia.

Sources: American Hotel & Lodging Association, Smith Travel Research

as a deposit or guarantee. Once the paperwork is done, room keys or key cards are issued, and guests are directed to their rooms.

Serve as primary guest liaison. Desk clerks often act as a buffer between the hotel and the guest. When guests have problems, have special requests, or encounter difficulties, they usually turn to the most visible person for help—the desk clerk. Some services provided to guests are laundry and valet requests, wake-up calls, and delivery of mail or messages. Clerks may also provide general information regarding the hotel or surrounding community. Their most important task, however, is to quickly address requests and complaints or to redirect the guest to the proper department.

Process guest departures. In some lodging establishments, a guest can choose to settle his or her account while in the room via the express, or video, checkout. Room charges are tallied on screen and charged to the customer's credit card. Desk clerks settle video checkouts at the end of the day and send folios to the guest's home address. However, many people still choose to personally check out at the front desk. After verifying and explaining all room charges, the desk clerk can begin to settle the guest's account. Sometimes, if credit authorization is declined, the clerk may have to politely negotiate an alternate method of payment. After thanking the guest and listening to any comments, positive or negative, the desk clerk can move on to the next customer or task.

Front office workers are responsible for keeping the hotel's information systems up to date. Many hotels now keep detailed information on their guests—such as the reason for their stay, their likes, and dislikes—and use this information for future marketing needs.

Depending on the type or size of the hotel, they may also be responsible for working the switchboard, bookkeeping, house banks and petty cash, daily bank deposits, and recoding key cards. In addition, they must keep the front desk area clean and presentable.

REQUIREMENTS

High School

In high school take classes such as business, marketing, and even psychology to prepare for this people-oriented job. Be sure to take English and speech courses to hone your communications skills. Lynda Witry, front desk supervisor at the Giorgios Hotel and Conference Center in Orland Park, Illinois, found her high school computer and typing classes helpful. "Being able to type—not the hunt-and-peck method—makes working on the computer faster." According to Witry, it also helps to know how to compute percentages and discounts quickly, so math skills are essential.

Postsecondary Training

If you are hoping to use a desk clerk job as a stepping-stone to a management position, you should consider a degree in hotel management. College courses that will be helpful to your career include human relations, finance, and practical classes such as hospitality supervision and front office procedures.

Internships are a great way to earn work experience, course credit, and most importantly, a chance to distinguish yourself from other applicants during an interview. Check with your high school guidance counselor or career center for a listing of available hospitality internships and schools that have two- or four-year programs, or contact the American Hotel & Lodging Educational Institute.

Certification or Licensing

Certification is not required for the position of desk clerk, though many consider it a measure of industry knowledge and experience. Programs such as those offered by the American Hotel & Lodging Educational Institute are designed to help improve job performance and advancement potential and keep you up to date on industry changes. Contact the institute for more information.

High school juniors and seniors who are interested in working in the hospitality industry can take advantage of the American Hotel & Lodging Educational Institute's Lodging Management Program. The program combines classroom learning with work experience in the hospitality industry. Graduating seniors who pass examinations and work in the lodging industry for at least 30 days receive the certified rooms division specialist designation. Visit http://www.lodging management.org for more information.

Other Requirements

"Desk clerks should be great communicators," says Witry. "They need to be able to deal with different kinds of people to be successful in this job." Organization, flexibility, and patience are some qualities needed when handling different situations and tasks simultaneously. You should be courteous and eager to help, even at times when the guests are demanding. When unable to help, you must be able to relay the guests' demands to the proper department. As a desk clerk, you will spend the majority of the day on your feet, so you should be in good physical condition. Computer knowledge, good phone manners, and readable penmanship are desirable for this job. Fluency in other languages, though not a requirement, is a great plus.

Good grooming habits are essential for this high visibility job. Strive for a professional look. Industry "don'ts" include unkempt or shocking hairstyles, excessive jewelry, and heavy or dramatic makeup. Desk clerks usually wear uniforms that are provided by the hotel and sometimes cleaned free of charge.

EXPLORING

The best way to explore this industry is to work in a hotel after school or during summer vacations. Although you may not land a desk clerk position, you may be hired as a waiter, waitress, dining-room attendant, or for a housekeeping position. You will be able to talk to people in the industry and learn the pros and cons of each job. If you can't find a job in the hotel industry, you might consider asking your school counselor to arrange an information interview with someone working in the field.

EMPLOYERS

Approximately 219,000 hotel, motel, and resort desk clerks are employed in the United States. Because hotels and motels are found worldwide, job opportunities for desk clerks are plentiful. The amount of responsibility given to a desk clerk depends on the size and type of lodging establishment. Larger hotels (usually located in busy urban areas), such as the 665-room Sheraton Manhattan in New York, may have separate departments, each responsible for answering phones, making advance reservations, or processing guest arrivals. The pace of work may be more frenzied at times because of the higher guest count. The Best Western Golden Buff Lodge in Boulder, Colorado, a hotel on the small side, may have to combine departments to accommodate a smaller staff.

STARTING OUT

Many jobs are posted in newspaper want ads, trade magazines, or hotel employee newsletters. Hoteljobs.com is a Web site where you can post your resume and search for jobs nationwide. High school career centers and their counselors are helpful in providing guidance, handbooks, and literature to interested students. They may even post part-time or seasonal work available in the field.

Hiring requirements vary by employer, but most hotels look for candidates with work experience as well as education. Many desk clerks have a high school diploma or the equivalent; but those ambitious enough to someday pursue the management track should consider obtaining an associate's or bachelor's degree in hotel management or a similar program. When applying for a job, experience in the hotel industry is a definite plus, although experience in the restaurant trade, customer service, or retail is equally valuable.

ADVANCEMENT

Desk clerks and reservation clerks are both considered entry-level positions. Promotions within the front office could lead to jobs as front desk supervisor or front office manager. Further advancement may be to the position of assistant hotel manager. It is also possible to move to other departments within the hotel, such as banquets or the sales department. Job promotions, especially to the management level, will be easier to obtain with further education.

EARNINGS

According to the U.S. Department of Labor, median annual earnings of hotel, motel, and resort desk clerks were $18,950 in 2007. The lowest paid 10 percent of these workers earned less than $14,480 per year, while the highest paid 10 percent made $27,890 or more annually. Salaries depend on the size, type, and location of the hotel.

After a probationary period, usually 90 days, front office workers frequently are offered medical and sometimes dental insurance, vacation and sick days, paid holidays, and employee discounts. Many companies offer employees several free nights' stay per year at any of their properties.

WORK ENVIRONMENT

The front desk is located inside the hotel lobby, which is often clean and well decorated for the benefit of the guests. Desk clerks are on their feet most of the day, greeting guests and processing the paperwork needed for check-ins and check-outs. Most full-time desk clerks work a normal eight-hour day. However, because hotels are open 24 hours a day, it may be necessary for new employees with little seniority to work less-desirable shifts. Some holiday work should be expected. Twenty percent of clerks work part time.

This industry, as a rule, tends to have a high turnover rate. Larger hotels, especially those located in busy urban areas, may offer opportunities for rapid advancement. Job openings are created as people climb the corporate ladder or leave the workforce for other reasons.

OUTLOOK

According to the *Occupational Outlook Handbook*, employment of hotel desk clerks is expected to grow faster than the average for all careers through 2016. The economic recession has had an effect on both business and pleasure travel, although some recovery is expected within the next several years. This trend may affect employment of desk clerks, but people still need to travel for business and pleasure. Consequently, dependable desk clerks will be needed to work the front desk, and reservation clerks will be needed to sell the rooms.

Jobs will be most plentiful with hotels located in busy urban areas, where there tend to be higher turnover rates. Larger hotels are known to pay higher wages, promote faster, and be more open to sending employees to further education classes and seminars. Downsides to working in a hotel in a big city include a high cost of living, which will probably eat up the pay difference that such a setting can provide. Also, employees of large-staffed hotels may tend to experience less camaraderie among coworkers.

Most skills needed to be a good desk clerk are learned on the job. On-site training is a common method of continuing education, though hotels may choose to send their management-track employees to off-site seminars or continuing education classes.

FOR MORE INFORMATION

For information on careers and educational opportunities, contact
American Hotel and Lodging Association
1201 New York Avenue, NW, Suite 600
Washington, DC 20005-3931

Tel: 202-289-3100
Email: informationcenter@ahla.com
http://www.ahla.com

For career and certification information, contact
American Hotel & Lodging Educational Institute
800 North Magnolia Avenue, Suite 300
Orlando, FL 32803-3261
Tel: 800-752-4567
http://www.ei-ahla.org

For information on scholarships, contact
American Hotel and Lodging Foundation
1201 New York Avenue, NW, Suite 600
Washington, DC 20005-3931
Tel: 202-289-3100
http://www.ahlef.org

For a listing of schools with programs in hotel management, contact
**International Council on Hotel, Restaurant, and Institutional
 Education**
2810 North Parham Road, Suite 230
Richmond, VA 23294-4422
Tel: 804-346-4800
http://chrie.org

Insurance Policy Processing Workers

QUICK FACTS

School Subjects
Business
Computer science
Mathematics

Personal Skills
Following instructions
Leadership/management

Work Environment
Primarily indoors
Primarily one location

Minimum Education Level
High school diploma

Salary Range
$21,950 to $32,040 to
$48,260+

Certification or Licensing
None available

Outlook
Little or no change

DOT
219

GOE
09.03.01

NOC
1434

O*NET-SOC
13-1031.01, 43-9041.00,
43-9041.01, 43-9041.02

OVERVIEW

Insurance policy processing workers perform a variety of clerical and administrative tasks that ensure that insurance applications and claims are handled in an efficient and timely manner. They review new applications, make adjustments to existing policies, work on policies that are to be reinstated, check the accuracy of company records, verify client information, and compile information used in claim settlements. Insurance policy processing personnel also handle business correspondence relating to any of the above duties. They use computers, word processors, calculators, and other office equipment in their work. There are approximately 254,000 insurance policy processing workers employed in the United States.

HISTORY

Organized insurance was first developed in the shipping industry during the late 1600s as a means of sharing the risks of commercial voyages. Underwriters received a fee for the portion of the financial responsibility they covered.

As the need for further protection developed, other types of insurance were created. After the London Fire of 1666, fire insurance became available in England. Life insurance first appeared in the United States in 1759, accident insurance followed in 1863, and automobile insurance was instituted in 1898.

Now, millions of dollars worth of insurance policies are written every day. Skilled claims examiners, medical-voucher clerks, and other insurance workers are needed to process applications and claims accurately and efficiently so clients get the coverage to which they are entitled.

THE JOB

Insurance policy processing workers are involved in all aspects of handling insurance applications and settling claims (or requests from policy owners regarding payment). The individual policies are sold by an *insurance agent* or *broker*, who sends the policies to processing workers and waits to see whether the company accepts the policy under the terms as written. The agent or the customer may contact policy-processing workers many times during the life of a policy for various services. *Claims examiners* review settled insurance claims to verify that payments have been made according to company procedures and are in line with the information provided in the claim form. These professionals may also need to contact policy processing clerks in the course of reviewing settlements. While a policy processing worker may be assigned a variety of tasks, insurance companies increasingly rely on specialists to perform specific functions.

Claims clerks review insurance claim forms for accuracy and completeness. Frequently, this involves calling or writing the insured party or other people involved to secure missing information. After placing this data in a claims file, the clerk reviews the insurance policy to determine the coverage. Routine claims are transmitted for payment; if further investigation is needed, the clerk informs the claims supervisor.

Claims supervisors not only direct the work of claims clerks but are also responsible for informing policy owners and beneficiaries of the procedures for filing claims. They submit claim liability statements for review by the actuarial department and inform department supervisors of the status of claims.

Reviewers check completed insurance applications to ensure that applicants have answered all questions. They contact insurance agents to inform them of any problems with the applications; if they don't find any problems, reviewers advise that policies be approved and delivered to applicants. Reviewers may collect premiums from new policy owners and provide management with updates on new business.

Policy-change clerks compile information on changes in insurance policies, such as a change in beneficiaries, and determine if the proposed changes conform to company policy and state law. Using rate books and their own knowledge of specific types of policies, these clerks calculate new premiums and make appropriate adjustments to accounts. Policy-change clerks may help write a new policy with the client's specified changes or prepare a rider to an existing policy.

Cancellation clerks cancel insurance policies as directed by insurance agents. They compute any refund due and mail any appropriate refund and the cancellation notice to the policy owner. Clerks also notify the bookkeeping department of the cancellation and send a notice to the insurance agent.

Revival clerks approve reinstatement of customers' insurance policies if the reason for the lapse in service, such as an overdue premium, is corrected within a specified time limit. They compare answers given by the policy owner on the reinstatement application with those previously approved by the company, and they examine company records to see if there are any circumstances that make reinstatement impossible. Revival clerks calculate the irregular premium and the reinstatement penalty due when the reinstatement is approved, type notices of company action (approval or denial of reinstatement), and send these notifications to the policy owner.

Insurance checkers verify the accuracy and completeness of insurance company records by comparing the computations on premiums paid and dividends due on individual forms. They then check that information against similar information on other applications. They also verify personal information on applications, such as the name, age, address, and value of property of the policy owner, and they proofread all material concerning insurance coverage before it is sent to policy owners.

Insurance agents must apply to insurance companies in order to represent the companies and sell their policies. *Agent-contract clerks* evaluate the ability and character of prospective insurance agents and approve or reject their contracts to sell insurance for a company. Among other things, they review the prospective agent's application for relevant work experience and check the applicant's personal references to see if they meet company standards. Agent-contract clerks correspond with both the prospective agent and company officials to explain their decision to accept or reject individual applications.

Medical-voucher clerks analyze vouchers sent by doctors who have completed medical examinations of insurance applicants and approve payment of these vouchers based on standard rates. These clerks note the doctor's fee on a form and forward the form and the voucher to the insurance company's bookkeeper or other appropriate personnel for further approval and payment.

REQUIREMENTS

High School

A high school diploma is usually sufficient for beginning insurance policy processing workers. To prepare yourself for this job, you should take courses in English, mathematics, and computer science while in high school. In addition, take as many business-related courses as possible, such as typing, word processing, and bookkeeping.

Postsecondary Training

Community colleges and vocational schools often offer business education courses that provide training for insurance policy processing workers. You may want to consider taking these courses to improve your possibilities for advancement to supervisory positions.

Other Requirements

To succeed in this field, you should have some aptitude with business machines, the ability to concentrate on repetitious tasks for long periods of time, and good math skills. Legible handwriting is a necessity. Because you will often work with policy owners and other workers, you must be able to communicate effectively and work well with others. In addition, insurance policy processing workers need to be familiar with state and federal insurance laws and regulations. They should find systematic and orderly work appealing, and they should like to work on detailed tasks.

Other personal qualifications include dependability, trustworthiness, and a neat personal appearance. Insurance policy processing personnel who work for the federal government may need to pass a civil service examination.

EXPLORING

You can get experience in this field by assuming clerical or bookkeeping responsibilities for a school club or other organization. In addition, some school work-study programs may have opportunities with insurance companies for part-time, on-the-job training. You might also get a part-time or summer job with an insurance company.

You can get training in office procedures and the operation of business machinery and computers through evening courses offered by business schools. Another way to gain insight into the responsibilities of insurance policy processing workers is to talk to someone already working in the field.

EMPLOYERS

Approximately 254,000 insurance claims and policy processing clerks are employed in the United States. Insurance companies are the principal employers of insurance policy processing workers. These workers may perform similar duties for real estate firms and the government.

STARTING OUT

If you are interested in securing an entry-level position, you should contact insurance agencies directly. Jobs may also be located through help-wanted advertisements or by visiting industry-related Web sites. Some insurance companies may give you an aptitude test to determine your ability to work quickly and accurately. Work assignments may be made on the basis of the results of this test.

ADVANCEMENT

Many inexperienced workers begin as file clerks and advance to positions in policy processing. Insurance policy processing workers usually begin their employment handling the more routine tasks, such as reviewing insurance applications to ensure that all the questions have been answered. With experience, they may advance to more complicated tasks and assume a greater responsibility for complete assignments. Those who show the desire and ability may be promoted to clerical supervisory positions, with a corresponding increase in pay and work responsibilities. To become a claims adjuster or an underwriter, it is usually necessary to have a college degree or have taken specialized courses in insurance. Many such courses are available from local business or vocational colleges and various industry trade groups.

The high turnover rate among insurance policy processing workers increases opportunities for promotions. The number and kind of opportunities, however, may depend on the place of employment and the ability, training, and experience of the employee.

EARNINGS

Insurance policy processing workers' salaries vary depending on such factors as a worker's experience and the size and location of the employer. Generally, those working for large companies in big cities earn higher salaries. According to the U.S. Department of Labor, the median yearly income for insurance policy processing clerks was

$32,040 in 2007. Salaries ranged from less than $21,950 to $48,260 or more.

As full-time employees of insurance companies, policy processing workers usually receive the standard fringe benefits of vacation and sick pay, health insurance, and retirement plans.

WORK ENVIRONMENT

As is the case with most office workers, insurance policy processing employees work an average of 37 to 40 hours a week. Although the work environment is usually well ventilated and lighted, the job itself can be fairly routine and repetitive, with most of the work taking place at a desk. Policy processing workers often interact with other insurance professionals and policyholders, and they may work under close supervision.

Because many insurance companies offer 24-hour claims service to their policyholders, some claims clerks may work evenings and weekends. Many insurance workers are employed part-time or on a temporary basis.

OUTLOOK

The U.S. Department of Labor predicts little or no employment change for insurance processing workers through 2016. Increased use of data processing machines and other types of automated equipment will increase worker productivity and result in the need for fewer workers.

Many jobs will result from workers retiring or otherwise leaving the field. Employment opportunities should be best in and around large metropolitan areas, where the majority of large insurance companies are located. There should be an increase in the number of opportunities for temporary or part-time work, especially during busy business periods.

FOR MORE INFORMATION

For information on educational programs, contact
Insurance Institute of America/American Institute for CPCU
720 Providence Road, Suite 100
Malvern, PA 19355-3433
Tel: 800-644-2101
Email: customerservice@cpcuiia.org
http://www.aicpcu.org

For information on career opportunities in Canada, contact
Insurance Institute of Canada
18 King Street East, 6th Floor
Toronto, ON M5C 1C4, Canada
Tel: 416-362-8586
Email: IICmail@insuranceinstitute.ca
http://www.insuranceinstitute.ca

Legal Secretaries

OVERVIEW

Legal secretaries, sometimes called *litigation secretaries* or *trial secretaries*, assist lawyers by performing the administrative and clerical duties in a law office or firm. Legal secretaries spend most of their time writing legal correspondence, preparing legal documents, performing research, and answering incoming calls and emails. Legal secretaries read and review many law journals to check for any new court decisions that may be important for cases pending at that time. Legal secretaries also maintain files and records, take notes during meetings or hearings, and assume all other general secretarial duties. Approximately 275,000 legal secretaries work in law offices and firms in the United States today.

HISTORY

Over the years the law has become increasingly complex. Along with that fact, more and more litigation proceedings have occurred which have led to the need for lawyers, first, to explain the law, and second, to pursue its defense. Originally, lawyers hired secretaries for their small, one- or two-lawyer office to assist with general clerical duties. Typing letters, filing documents, and receiving clients were the main duties of these general secretaries. As lawyers were forced to spend more of their time dealing with the difficulties of the law and with their increased number of clientele, secretaries were given more responsibility. The secretaries were transformed from being mainly receptionists to managing the law office, at least the administrative side of it. Lawyers started to look to their secretaries more as legal assistants than receptionists. Today legal secretaries are indispensable to most lawyers and play a major role in each client's case by streamlining all documentation, communication, and research into a usable source of information.

The legal secretary field has also grown in this computer age. "As an example of how information technology has transformed the profession, 20 years ago the rule was 'one lawyer, one secretary,'" says professional legal secretary Alexis Montgomery. "Now with computer word processing, specialized programs for legal practices, and information technology in all of its forms, typically one experienced legal secretary can handle two lawyers." Although most computer advances have helped the legal secretary field expand, some lawyers are using this technology to increase their own productivity. The lawyer can reassume some duties that the legal secretary does now—reducing the need for secretaries.

Although lawyers may be more computer-savvy, legal secretaries still play an important, but changing role. For example, whereas before the legal secretary took dictation, typed out a letter, and then proofread it for accuracy, now the lawyer may type his or her own letter on the computer and ask the legal secretary to edit it and to fact check some of the main points. Lawyers aren't the only ones taking advantage of new technology; legal secretaries now have the advantage of using personal computers instead of electronic typewriters, and fax machines instead of telex machines. The World Wide Web has made research much easier as well.

THE JOB

Legal secretaries must be able to handle all the duties of a general secretary plus all the specific responsibilities that come with working for a lawyer. Although every law office or firm may vary in the exact duties required for the position, in general, most legal secretaries spend their time managing information that comes in and goes out of the law office. "No one day is the same with my job," says Julie Abernathy, a legal secretary at Haynes and Boone, LLP in Austin, Texas. "That in itself is what I love most about my career. Each case is different from the next, and each client is unique in their/its own way. I typically interact with the clients, prepare correspondence, transmitting pleadings and documents to opposing counsel, court house personnel, and clients for review and approval. My supervising attorneys do not give me specific instructions, as they know I am very familiar with procedures and responsibilities with my job. I also assist my attorneys with basic research, document retrieval, document production, and even with their travel arrangements."

Legal secretaries may type letters and legal documents, such as sub-poenas, appeals, and motions; handle incoming and outgoing mail; maintain a detailed filing system; and deliver legal documents to the court. Besides these duties, legal secretaries spend much of their time making appointments with clients and dealing with client questions. "An important part of being an effective legal secretary is fielding telephone calls and all client contact efficiently and courteously," says Alexis Montgomery. "Often the client's primary contact is with the legal secretary and client satisfaction depends heavily on how helpful and courteous that contact is perceived." The legal secretary is a personal assistant to one or more lawyers as well, maintaining the calendars and schedules for the office. "Always knowing where your attorney can be found or whether another attorney can assist the client is an important part of the process," says Montgomery.

Legal secretaries are also called upon to conduct research for current cases. They may research and write legal briefs on a topic or case that is relevant to the lawyer's current cases. According to Rebecca Garland, a legal advocate who was trained as a legal secretary but is now using those skills to assist victims of domestic violence in obtaining personal protection orders, research often takes up an entire workday. "You may spend one whole day working on a legal brief for one client, and then spend the next day working on small things for several different cases." Legal secretaries spend many hours researching cases in law libraries, public libraries, and on the

A legal secretary researches land records at a government office.
(Bob Daemmrich/The Image Works)

Internet. Part of this research includes scouring legal journals and magazines looking for relevant laws and courtroom decisions that may affect the clientele.

Legal secretaries are also record keepers. They help lawyers find information such as employment, medical, and criminal records. They also keep records from all previous clients and court cases for future use. Legal secretaries must also track and use various forms, such as trial request, client application, and accident report forms. "The bottom line is that legal secretaries process the paperwork generated by their attorneys," says Alexis Montgomery.

REQUIREMENTS

High School
Because a legal secretary must be able to communicate the attorney's ideas in written and oral form, it's important to get a firm grounding in English (especially writing), spelling, typing, and public speaking. Computers are used in most law offices, so be sure to gain computer experience while in high school. Government and political science courses will get you started on the road to legal knowledge. Classes that give you experience with research are also important. Rebecca Garland says, "Learning how to do research in the school or community library will go a long way in learning how to do research in a law library."

Postsecondary Training
Many legal secretaries get their training through established one- or two-year legal secretary programs. These programs are available at most business, vocational, and junior colleges. You could also obtain a four-year degree to get a well-rounded education. Courses taken should focus on specific skills and knowledge needed by a legal secretary, such as personal computers, keyboarding, English, legal writing, editing, researching, and communication. NALS...the association for legal professionals also offers basic and advanced legal secretary training courses.

As businesses continue to expand worldwide, employers are increasingly looking for candidates with bachelor's degrees and professional certifications.

Certification or Licensing
Two general legal secretary certifications are offered by NALS...the association for legal professionals. After some preliminary office training, you can take an examination to receive the accredited legal secretary designation. This certification is for legal secretaries with

education, but little to no experience. Legal secretaries with three years of experience can become certified as a professional legal secretary (PLS). The PLS certification designates a legal secretary with exceptional skills and experience.

Other specific legal secretary certifications are given by Legal Secretaries International. You can become board certified in civil litigation, probate, real estate, business law, criminal law, or intellectual property. Applicants must have a minimum of five years of law experience and pass an examination.

Other Requirements

To be employed as a legal secretary, you must learn a great deal of legal terminology and court structures and practices. Whether through study or experience, you must be able to grasp the inner workings of the law. "Excellent grammar and composition skills are two of the most important attributes needed for this profession," advises Patricia Infanti, a legal secretary with more than 30 years of experience. In addition, you must also be able to quickly learn computer programs, especially word processing and database programs, and be able to use them skillfully. "Students interested in this career need to know their way around the keyboard," says Infanti. "They should also know basic and advanced applications in Microsoft Word, Outlook, Excel, and PowerPoint." The ability to prioritize and balance different tasks is also necessary for the job. Legal secretaries must be organized and focused to handle their varying responsibilities.

EXPLORING

If this career interests you, suggest a career day at your school (if one isn't already scheduled) where professionals from a variety of careers give presentations. Be sure to let your career counselor know that you would like to have a legal secretary come as a guest speaker. Or you can ask your political science or government teacher to take your class on a field trip to a law library. Many law offices hire "runners" to deliver and file documents. Check with local law offices and offer your services for the summer or after school. You may also find it helpful to contact a local law firm and ask a legal secretary there if you can conduct an information interview.

EMPLOYERS

Approximately 275,000 legal secretaries are employed in the United States. The majority of legal secretaries work for law offices or law firms. Some government agencies on the state and national level also employ legal secretaries. More law firms and offices are located in Washington, D.C., and in larger metropolitan areas, so these regions offer more opportunities. However, most law offices and firms are now online. The Internet enables workers to send information easily from the law office to the courtroom, so offices are not forced to be located close to the courts. Legal secretaries are in demand anywhere lawyers practice.

STARTING OUT

Many legal secretaries get their first job through the career services offices of their college or vocational school. Still other legal secretaries start by working part time, gaining experience toward a first full-time position. Alexis Montgomery started out that way: "My first employment was as a staff secretary on a newspaper. Thereafter I worked as a 'floater' in a medium-sized law firm. (A *floater* is a secretary who is not assigned to any particular lawyer, but fills in for absent secretaries and handles overflow.) This job was my first exposure to the field and provided on-the-job training as a legal secretary." Montgomery also adds that working as a floater exposes you to a wide variety of legal practices—useful when deciding which area you want to specialize in. Don't forget to contact the local law offices in your area and let them know you are available; often direct contact now can lead to a job later.

ADVANCEMENT

Experienced legal secretaries are often promoted to oversee less experienced legal secretaries. Some firms have senior legal secretaries who are given more responsibility and less supervision duties. "In many cases more experienced legal secretaries do the drafting of letters and documents and pass them on to the attorney for revision or signature," says Alexis Montgomery. "As one becomes more experienced and proficient, the work of a legal secretary tends to blend into what is regarded as paralegal work." Legal secretaries may continue their education and become paralegals themselves. Many of the skills legal secretaries obtain can be transferred to almost any other office setting.

EARNINGS

According to the U.S. Department of Labor, the average salary for legal secretaries was approximately $38,810 in 2007. Salaries ranged from less than $24,380 to more than $60,800. An attorney's rank in the firm will also affect the salary of his or her legal secretary;

secretaries who work for a partner will earn higher salaries than those who work for an associate. Certified legal secretaries generally receive higher pay.

Most law firms provide employees with sick days, vacation days, and holidays. Health insurance, 401(k) plans, and profit sharing may be offered as well. Some law firms offer in-house training or pay for off-site classes to increase their secretarial skills.

WORK ENVIRONMENT

Legal secretaries spend the majority of their day behind their desk at a computer. They spend lengthy periods of time typing or writing, which may cause hand and wrist strain. Long hours staring at a computer monitor may also cause eyestrain. Legal secretaries work with lawyers, other legal secretaries, clients, court personnel, library personnel, and other support workers. Senior legal secretaries supervise some legal secretaries; others are left largely unsupervised. Most legal secretaries are full-time employees who work a 40-hour week. Some are part-time workers who move into full-time status as they gain more experience. Because the legal secretary's work revolves around the lawyer, many secretaries work long hours of overtime.

Legal secretaries may work at small, single attorney firms, mid-sized firms, or large law firms with offices throughout the United States. Patricia Infanti works at Ballard Spahr Andrews & Ingersoll, LLP, a large law firm with 10 offices. "Working for a large firm is a wonderful opportunity because large firms offer so many benefits and services that a small law firm simply cannot afford," she explains. "Not only is my work space well laid out with a large wrap-around desk and comfortable chair, but my printer is next to my desk and other office machines are close by. When I have computer difficulties, I have an entire department available to immediately assist me. In addition, there is a print room, mail room, and other services, which enable me to concentrate on my attorneys' work."

OUTLOOK

Because the legal services industry as a whole is growing, legal secretaries are in demand. An increased need for lawyers in such areas as intellectual property cases will leave lawyers in need of assistance with their caseloads. Qualified legal secretaries will have plentiful job opportunities, especially in the larger metropolitan areas.

Technological advances have revolutionized traditional secretarial tasks such as typing or keeping correspondence. The use of email, scanners, and the Internet will make secretaries more productive in coming years. Although the efficient use of technology has decreased the need for secretaries in some professions, it has only expanded the responsibilities for secretaries. According to the *Occupational Outlook Handbook*, employment for legal secretaries will grow about as fast as the average for all occupations through 2016. "The role of 'legal secretary' may change throughout the years, but it will never phase out," predicts Julie Abernathy. "I can only imagine what my job will be like in the next 10 to 15 years and am looking forward to learning new things."

FOR MORE INFORMATION

For information about certification, careers, and job listings, contact
    Legal Secretaries International
    2302 Fannin Street, Suite 500
    Houston, TX 77002-9136
    http://www.legalsecretaries.org

For information on certification, job openings, a variety of careers in law, and more, contact
    NALS...the association for legal professionals
    8159 East 41st Street
    Tulsa, OK 74145-3313
    Tel: 918-582-5188
    Email: info@nals.org
    http://www.nals.org

═══════════════ INTERVIEW ═══════════════

Patricia Infanti is a legal secretary at Ballard Spahr Andrews & Ingersoll, LLP, a large law firm with 10 offices. She is also the education director of NALS . . . the association for legal professionals. Patricia discussed her career with the editors of Careers in Focus: Clerks and Administrative Workers.

Q. How long have you been a legal secretary? How did you get into the field?

A. I have been a legal secretary since 1977. When I was in high school, I did not study office procedures and had to take those courses in community college. I graduated in 1977 with an associate's degree in executive secretarial science. I was unable to enter the college's Legal Secretarial Science program because I did not have the shorthand prerequisite needed to do so.

After graduating from college, I worked in a small, five-attorney law office as the assistant to the office manager/legal secretary to the founding partner. I worked at my first law firm for seven years, my second law firm (also a small firm with six attorneys) for six years, and my current law firm, Ballard Spahr Andrews & Ingersoll, LLP, for the last 18 years. I work with two well-known real estate attorneys, one of whom I've been with for more than 12 years. The atmosphere of my department is pleasant, and all of us consider ourselves professionals and work well with each other. I feel confident in saying that I will probably stay with this firm until I retire.

Q. What were your expectations entering this field? Were they much different from the realities?

A. I did not know what to expect upon entering the legal field. My schooling prepared me for work in a business office. Consequently, I had to quickly learn all of the legal aspects of a law office. I was fortunate that the office manager/legal secretary was actually looking for someone with no legal knowledge that she could train to do things her way. This consummate professional taught me everything from what it means to be a legal secretary, to court procedures, to law office accounting, to how to work with court personnel, other legal secretaries, and clients. She taught me all I needed to know about this service-oriented profession.

What was surprising to me were the amount of details that were part of the legal profession. I had to learn how to prepare documents in conformance with various judges' preferences and how to work well with court staff so that I could get things done promptly and properly. At one time I considered continuing my education to become an attorney. However, I realized that my strengths were in my organizational skills and my ability to remember details and incorporate them into my work.

Q. How and where did you get your first job in this field? What did you do?

A. In the summer of 1977, after graduation from college, I learned of the position I described earlier through a coworker where I was working. I called for an interview and took a substantial cut in pay (I was an assistant department manager in a retail store) in order to get my foot in the door. It was difficult even then to get a job without experience so I knew I needed to learn quickly. I have never regretted my decision to move into the legal field.

Q. What advice would you give to high school students who are interested in becoming legal secretaries?

A. The most important advice I would give is not to discount the challenges and variety of the legal secretarial profession. What I do is an intricate part of this law firm, and my attorneys would not be able to accomplish all that they do without me. So many young people believe that being a "secretary" is less than being a "paralegal." But that is not the case. In fact, every day is different, with its own situations and challenges. I have become quite adept in finding solutions to keep my attorneys' practices running smoothly—I am the clearinghouse, coordinating the efforts of other departments to get my attorneys' work completed correctly and in a timely manner.

Participating in any club or in student government (especially as secretary) would provide an excellent learning experience that would prepare them for the legal services profession. Participating in an English club or the school newspaper would help with language skills. Also, students should participate in ethics seminars or programs if those are available. I would also encourage participation in office internships through school-to-work programs, which would provide valuable office experience.

Library Technicians

OVERVIEW

Library technicians, sometimes called *library technical assistants*, work in all areas of library services, supporting professional librarians or working independently to help people access information. They order and catalog books, help library patrons locate materials, and make the library's services and facilities accessible. Technicians verify bibliographic information on orders and perform basic cataloging of materials received. They answer routine questions about library services and refer questions requiring professional help to librarians. Technicians also help with circulation desk operations and oversee the work of stacks workers, library aides, and other clerical workers. They circulate audiovisual equipment and materials and inspect items upon return. Approximately 121,000 library technicians are employed in the United States.

HISTORY

The earliest libraries, referred to in Egyptian manuscripts, date from 3000 B.C. The centuries since have seen great changes in libraries and their place in society. In the Middle Ages books were so rare that they were often chained to shelves to prevent loss. The inventions of the printing press and movable type increased the literacy rate, and the increasing availability of books and periodicals all contributed to the growth of libraries.

The growth of public education in the 1800s was accompanied by a rapid growth of public libraries across the United States, greatly aided in the latter part of the century by the generosity of philanthropists such as Andrew Carnegie. Cataloging systems and other aids to locating information were developed, such as the Dewey

Decimal System in 1876 and *Poole's Index to Periodical Literature* in 1882; these aids made libraries much more convenient for users. The American Library Association was founded in 1876, an event that is usually regarded as marking the birth of librarianship as a profession.

The great increase in the amount of recorded information in the 20th century has led to a steady increase in the number of library facilities and services. It is estimated that the amount of information published on almost every general subject doubles every 10 to 20 years. Libraries depend on trained personnel to keep informed about what new information is available, to be selective about what materials are purchased, and to share materials with other libraries as an extension of their own resources.

As the responsibilities of librarians became more complex, the need for technically trained workers to support them became evident. During the 1940s many libraries began training their own support staff. Now that computers are used for many of the technical and user services, library technicians perform many of the tasks once handled exclusively by librarians.

THE JOB

Work in libraries falls into three general categories: technical services, user services, and administrative services. Library technicians may be involved with the responsibilities of any of these areas.

In technical services, library technicians are involved with acquiring resources and then organizing them so the material can be easily accessed. They process order requests, verify bibliographic information, and prepare order forms for new materials, such as books, magazines, journals, videos, digital video discs (DVDs), and CD-ROMs. They perform routine cataloging of new materials and record information about the new materials in computer files or on cards to be stored in catalog drawers. The *acquisitions technicians, classifiers,* and *catalogers* who perform these functions make information available for the library users. Technicians who work for interlibrary loan departments may arrange for one library to borrow materials from another library. Other technicians might make basic repairs to damaged books or refer the materials to a preservation department for more comprehensive conservation. A *circulation counter attendant* helps readers check out materials and collects late fines for overdue books. *Media technicians* operate audiovisual equipment for library media programs and maintain the equipment in working order.

Under the guidance of librarians in user services, technicians work directly with library patrons and help them to access the information needed for their research. They direct library patrons to the online catalog in response to inquiries and assist with identifying the library's holdings. They describe the general arrangement of the library for new patrons and answer basic questions about the library's collections. They may also help patrons use microfiche and microfilm equipment. They may help them locate materials in an interlibrary system's computerized listing of holdings. *Reference library technicians* specialize in locating and researching information. *Children's library technicians* and *young-adult library technicians* specialize in getting children and young adults interested in books, reading, and learning by sponsoring summer reading programs, reading hours, puppet shows, literacy contests, and other fun activities.

Technicians who work in administrative services help with the management of the library. They might help prepare budgets, coordinate the efforts of different departments within the library, write policy and procedures, and work to develop the library's collection. If they have more responsibility they might supervise and coordinate staff members, recruit and supervise volunteers, organize fundraising efforts, sit on community boards, and develop programs to promote and encourage reading and learning in the community.

The particular responsibilities of a library technician vary according to the type of library. *Academic library technicians* work in university or college libraries, assisting professors and students in their research needs. They handle reference materials and specialized journals. *School library technicians* work with *school library media specialists*, assisting teachers and students in utilizing the print and nonprint resources of a school library media center.

Library technicians also work in special libraries maintained by government agencies, corporations, law firms, advertising agencies, museums, professional associations, medical centers, religious organizations, and research laboratories. Library technicians in special libraries deal with information tailored to the specific needs and interests of the particular organization. They may also organize bibliographies, prepare abstracts and indexes of current periodicals, or research and analyze information on particular issues.

Library technicians develop and index computerized databases to organize information collected in the library. They also help library patrons use computers to access the information stored in their own databases or in remote databases. With the increasing use of automated information systems, many libraries hire *automated system technicians* to help plan and operate computer systems and *information technicians* to help design and develop information storage retrieval systems and procedures for collecting, organizing, interpreting, and classifying information.

Library Facts

- Americans check out more than 2 billion books, DVDs, and other resources from public libraries each year.
- The average public library patron checks out seven resources annually.
- Students make 1.5 billion visits to school library media centers each year.
- There are approximately 123,291 libraries of all kinds in the United States.
- The largest libraries (by volumes held) in the United States are 1) Library of Congress; 2) Harvard University; 3) Boston Public Library; 4) Yale University; and 5) Chicago Public Library.

Sources: National Center for Education Statistics, American Library Association

In the past library technicians functioned solely as the librarian's support staff, but this situation has evolved over the years. Library technicians continue to refer questions or problems requiring professional experience and judgment to librarians. However, with the increasing use of computer systems in libraries, library technicians now perform many of the technical and user service responsibilities once performed by librarians, thereby freeing librarians to focus more on acquisitions and administrative responsibilities. In some cases a library technician may handle the same responsibilities as a librarian, even in place of a librarian.

REQUIREMENTS

High School

If you are considering a career as a library technician, you should take a college preparatory course load. Classes in English, history, literature, foreign languages, computers, and mathematics are crucial to giving you a strong background in the skills you will need as a library technician. Strong verbal and writing skills are especially important, so take all the classes you can to help you develop facility in speaking and writing. Any special knowledge of a particular subject matter can also be beneficial. For instance, if you have a strong interest in geography, you may want to consider pursuing a technical assistant position in a map room of a library.

Postsecondary Training

The technical nature of the work performed by library technicians, especially when working in technical services, is prompting more and more libraries to hire only high school graduates who have gone on to complete a two-year program in library technology. Many enroll in a two-year certificate program that, upon graduation, bestows the title library technical assistant (LTA). Typical programs include courses in the basic purpose and functions of libraries; technical courses in processing materials, cataloging acquisitions, library services, and use of the Internet; and one year of liberal arts studies. Persons entering such programs should understand that the library-related courses they take will not apply toward a professional degree in library science.

For some positions, a bachelor's degree may be required in a specific area, such as art history for work in a museum library, or sociology for a position at a YMCA library. Specialized study in a foreign language may be helpful, since most libraries have materials in many languages, and all of those materials must be cataloged and processed for library patrons to use. Also, not all library users speak English; a library employee who is able to communicate with all users in person, via email, on the telephone, and in writing is especially effective. While in college, you will probably be required to take courses in the liberal arts: sociology, psychology, speech, history, and literature, among others.

Some smaller libraries, especially in rural communities, may hire persons with only a high school education for library technician positions. Some libraries may hire individuals who have prior work experience, and some may provide their own training for inexperienced individuals. On the other hand, some libraries may only hire library technicians who have earned associate's or bachelor's degrees.

Other Requirements

Whatever your educational or training background, you should demonstrate aptitude for careful, detailed, analytical work. You should enjoy problem solving and working with people as well as with books and other library materials. Good interpersonal skills are invaluable, since library technicians often have much public contact. As a library technician, you should possess patience and flexibility and should not mind being interrupted frequently to answer questions from library patrons.

You should also exhibit good judgment; you'll need to know when you can effectively assist a user and when the problem must be referred to a professional librarian. Since there are many tasks that must get done in order to make materials available to users, you must have excellent time management skills. Technicians who supervise the work of others must be able to manage effectively, explain procedures, set deadlines, and follow through with subordinates. You should also feel comfortable reporting to supervisors and working alongside other technicians in a team atmosphere.

EXPLORING

Personal experience as a library patron is the first opportunity for you to see if a library career would be of interest to you. You can get a good idea of the general atmosphere of a library by browsing for books, searching in electronic encyclopedias for a school research project, or using a library's Internet connection to access all kinds of information. Using libraries yourself will also give you an idea of the types of services that a library provides for its patrons.

If you are interested in a career as a library technician, talk with librarians and library technicians at your school or community library. A visit to a large or specialized library would also be helpful in providing a view of the different kinds of libraries that exist.

There may also be opportunities to work as a library volunteer at a public library or in the school library media center. Some grammar schools or high schools have library clubs as a part of their extracurricular activities. If your school doesn't have a library club, contact your school librarian and get some friends together to start your own group. Part-time or summer work as a shelving clerk or typist may also be available in some libraries.

EMPLOYERS

There are approximately 121,000 library technicians employed in the United States. Most library technicians work in grammar school, high school, college, university, and public libraries. Others work for government libraries (primarily at the Library of Congress and the U.S. Department of Defense), in special libraries for privately held institutions, and in corporate libraries. Many types of organizations employ library technicians. For example, library technicians are key personnel at archives, zoos, museums, hospitals, fraternal organizations, historical societies, medical centers, law firms, professional societies, advertising agencies, and virtual libraries. In general, wherever there is a library, library technicians are needed.

STARTING OUT

Since specific training requirements vary from library to library, if you are interested in a career as a library technician, you should be familiar with the requirements of the libraries in which you hope to work. In some small libraries, for instance, a high school diploma may be sufficient, and a technician might not need a college degree. However, since most libraries require their library technicians to be graduates of at least a two-year associate's degree program, you should have earned or be close to earning this degree before applying.

In most cases, graduates of training programs for library technicians may seek employment through the career services offices of their community colleges. Job applicants may also approach libraries directly, usually by contacting the personnel officer of the library or the human resources administrator of the organization. Civil service examination notices, for those interested in government service, are usually posted in community colleges as well as in government buildings and on government Web sites.

Many state library agencies maintain job hotlines listing openings for prospective library technicians. State departments of education also may keep lists of openings available for library technicians. If you are interested in working in a school library media center, you should remember that most openings occur at the end of the school year and are filled for the following year.

ADVANCEMENT

The trend toward requiring more formal training for library technicians suggests that advancement opportunities will be limited for those lacking such training. In smaller libraries and less-populated areas, the shortage of trained personnel may lessen this limitation. Nonetheless, those with adequate or above-average training will perform the more interesting tasks.

Generally, library technicians advance by taking on greater levels of responsibility. A new technician, for instance, may check materials in and out at the library's circulation desk and then move on to inputting, storing, and verifying information. Experienced technicians in supervisory roles might be responsible for budgets and personnel or the operation of an entire department. Library technicians will find that experience, along with continuing education courses, will enhance their chances for advancement.

Library technicians might also advance by pursuing a master's degree in library and information science and becoming a librarian. With experience, additional courses, or an advanced degree, technicians can also advance to higher paying positions outside of the library setting.

EARNINGS

Salaries for library technicians vary depending on such factors as the type of library, geographic location, and specific job responsibilities. According to the U.S. Department of Labor, the median annual salary for all library technicians in 2007 was $27,680. The lowest paid 10 percent made less than $16,430, while the highest paid 10 percent earned more than $44,350. The U.S. Department of Labor also reported that library technicians employed by the federal government had mean annual salaries of $42,220 in 2007.

Benefits vary according to employer, but most full-time library technicians receive the same benefits as other employees, which may include the following: health insurance, dental insurance, paid vacations, paid holidays, compensated sick time, and retirement savings plans. Library technicians in grammar schools and high schools generally work fewer hours during summers and holidays when students are not in class, although these "down" times are often used to finish up backlogged projects. Technicians who work in corporate libraries may receive special perks as part of their benefits plan, such as stock in the company or discounts on products the company produces or markets. Many colleges and universities offer their employees discounted or free classes to help them earn an advanced degree. Most employers offer training sessions to their technicians to keep them informed of new developments in library services and technology.

WORK ENVIRONMENT

Libraries usually have clean, well-lit, pleasant work atmospheres. Hours are regular in company libraries and in school library media centers, but academic, public, and some specialized libraries are open longer hours and may require evening and weekend work, usually on a rotating basis.

Some tasks performed by library technicians, like calculating circulation statistics, can be repetitive. Technicians working in technical services may develop headaches and eyestrain from working long hours in front of a computer screen. Heavy public contact in user services may test a technician's tact and patience. However, a library's atmosphere is generally relaxed and interesting. The size and type of library will often determine the duties of library technicians. A technician working in a small branch library might handle a wide range of responsibilities. Sometimes a technician working in a school, rural, or special library might be the senior staff member, with full responsibility for all technical, user, and administrative services and staff supervision. A technician working in a large university or public library might focus on only one task all of the time.

Libraries are presently responding to decreased government funding by cutting budgets and reducing staff, often leaving an overwhelming workload for the remaining staff members. Because library technicians earn less money than librarians do, libraries often replace librarians with technicians. This situation can lead to resentment in the working relationship among colleagues. In addition, there is also an ongoing struggle to define the different responsibilities of the librarian and technician. Despite the difference in the educational requirements for the two jobs—librarians require a master's degree and technicians an associate's degree—some of the responsibilities do overlap. Library technicians may find it frustrating that, in some cases, they are performing the same tasks as librarians and yet do not command as high a salary.

OUTLOOK

The U.S. Department of Labor predicts that employment for library technicians will grow about as fast as the average for all careers through 2016. Job openings will result from technicians leaving the field for other employment or retirement, as well as from libraries looking to stretch their budgets by hiring library technicians to handle computer-oriented tasks previously overseen by librarians. Since a library technician earns less than a librarian, a library may find it more economical to hire the technician. The continued growth of special libraries in medical, business, and law organizations will lead to growing opportunities for technicians who develop specialized skills. A technician who has excellent computer skills and is able to learn quickly will be highly employable, as will a technician who shows the drive to gain advanced degrees and accept more responsibility.

FOR MORE INFORMATION

For information on library technician careers in Canada, contact
Alberta Association of Library Technicians
Box 700
Edmonton, AB T5J 2L4 Canada
http://www.aalt.org

For information on library careers, accredited schools, scholarships and grants, and college student membership, contact
American Library Association
50 East Huron Street

Chicago, IL 60611-2729
Tel: 800-545-2433
Email: pio@ala.org
http://www.ala.org

For information on education and awards programs, contact
Association for Educational Communications and Technology
1800 North Stonelake Drive, Suite 2
Bloomington, IN 47404-1517
Tel: 877-677-2328
Email: aect@aect.org
http://www.aect.org

To request information on education programs in Canada and scholarships, contact
Canadian Library Association
328 Frank Street
Ottawa, ON K2P 0X8 Canada
Tel: 613-232-9625
Email: info@cla.ca
http://www.cla.ca

For information on continuing education programs and publications, contact
Library & Information Technology Association
c/o American Library Association
50 East Huron Street
Chicago, IL 60611-2795
Tel: 800-545-2433, ext. 4270
Email: lita@ala.org
http://www.lita.org

For information on the wide variety of careers in special libraries, contact
Special Libraries Association
331 South Patrick Street
Alexandria, VA 22314-3501
Tel: 703-647-4900
Email: sla@sla.org
http://www.sla.org

INTERVIEW

Robin Martindill is a library technician at San Diego Mesa College in San Diego, California. She discussed her career with the editors of Careers in Focus: Clerks and Administrative Workers.

Q. How long have you worked in the field?

A. I have been in the field for 11 years at three different community college libraries. I began as a clerk. I did clerical work for two years and was promoted to technician nine years ago. I first worked in collection management (overseeing shelving); in the same position I would monitor overdue fines and send notices as well. For the last six years I have worked in acquisitions.

Q. What made you want to become a library technician?

A. I have always loved order and organization—keeping things alphabetical or catalogued. I love the smell and feel of books. I enjoy reading and having information at my fingertips. I love computers and researching on the Internet. As a child I would visit the library of every city I was taken to and continue that today. I love the architecture of libraries and the history. I'm always curious about how libraries choose to organize their collections. I'm still undecided if I want to further my education and become a librarian.

Q. What are your primary and secondary job duties?

A. There are many facets to a library technician. Some primarily do cataloging, others collection management. Personally my primary job duty is acquisitions. I am responsible for purchasing books/materials for my library. I do this at the direction of a librarian; however, most institutions (mine included) give the technician autonomy to select titles. My secondary duty is circulation. This is where I assist patrons to find books and check items in and out. Circulation is the "information booth" of the library as well.

Q. What do you like most and least about your job?

A. Like most: I enjoy meeting the people mostly who come in to the library. We have a variance of patrons—from the first-time college student who sees the Library of Congress for the first time to the grandmother just coming in for an enrichment class (but needs to use the online catalog)—and I have the pleasure of assisting them. Equally I love being the first person to open a brand-new book and put the information about it in the computer to help our patrons find it.

Like least: I monitor budgets for various vendors that I purchase my books from. I'm not an accountant. No one likes to pay bills...especially me.

Q. **What advice would you give to high school students who are interested in this career?**

A. If you enjoy having things in order and organized and you have a love of books or research, working in a library can be a very fulfilling career. A library technician job can be a stepping-stone to bigger career goals such as a librarian or a great career in itself. There are many different libraries to serve—from law libraries to special collection libraries. Even Disney World has a library. Sometimes a technician works in a huge room with just books and other times assists multiple patrons in a busy setting. It's the type of job that gives you the best of both worlds.

Some areas that may help you in a library technician career: in high school you can be a library page or one who returns books to their proper location on the shelf. Involvement in book clubs or reading programs. Activities would include volunteering to read to children in a church setting or in their classes. In high school I volunteered to read to adults at a retirement home. (If I worked in a public library or elementary school library this story-telling experience would come in handy.)

Q. **What are the most important professional qualities for library technicians?**

A. As I said in response to almost every question it is extremely important to be able to organize and put things in order. Libraries today have online collections as well as print collections so it's important to be computer savvy. Depending on what type of library you choose to work in you may need skills working with and serving patrons with diverse backgrounds. Other professional qualities include being a self-starter, a self-motivator, and having an ability to work unsupervised.

Medical Record Technicians

OVERVIEW

In any hospital, clinic, or other health care facility, permanent records are created and maintained for all the patients treated by the staff. Each patient's medical record describes in detail his or her condition over time. Entries include illness and injuries, operations, treatments, outpatient visits, and the progress of hospital stays. *Medical record technicians* compile, code, and maintain these records. They also tabulate and analyze data from groups of records in order to assemble reports. They review records for completeness and accuracy; assign codes to the diseases, operations, diagnoses, and treatments according to detailed standardized classification systems; and post the codes on the medical record. They transcribe medical reports; maintain indices of patients, diseases, operations, and other categories of information; compile patient census data; and file records. In addition, they may direct the day-to-day operations of the medical records department. They maintain the flow of records and reports to and from other departments, and sometimes assist medical staff in special studies or research that draws on information in the records. There are approximately 170,000 medical record technicians employed in the United States.

QUICK FACTS

School Subjects
Biology
English

Personal Skills
Following instructions
Technical/scientific

Work Environment
Primarily indoors
Primarily one location

Minimum Education Level
Associate's degree

Salary Range
$19,690 to $29,290 to $75,000

Certification or Licensing
Recommended

Outlook
Faster than the average

DOT
079

GOE
09.07.02

NOC
1413

O*NET-SOC
29-2071.00

HISTORY

Medical practitioners have been recording information about their patients' illnesses and treatments for hundreds of years. Before the

20th and 21st centuries, such records were kept mostly to help the practitioners retain and learn as much as possible from their own experience. Because there was little centralization or standardization of this information, it was difficult to organize and share the knowledge that resulted from studying many instances of similar cases.

A medical record technician files patient charts. *(Scott Stulberg/Corbis)*

By the early 1900s medical record keeping was changing, along with many other aspects of health care. Medicine was more sophisticated, scientific, and successful in helping patients. Hospitals were increasingly becoming accepted as the conventional place for middle-class patients to go for care, and as a result, hospitals became more numerous and better organized. As hospitals grew larger and served more patients, the volume of patient records increased proportionately. With medical record keeping becoming more important and time consuming, it was most efficient and sensible to centralize it within the hospital. Recommendations by distinguished committees representing the medical profession also encouraged standardized record-keeping procedures.

By the 1920s many hospitals in the United States had central libraries of patient information, with employees specifically hired to keep these records in good order. As time passed, their tasks became more complicated. The employees responsible for this work, who used to be called medical record librarians, eventually became differentiated into two basic professional categories: medical record administrators and medical record technicians. In 1953 the first formal training programs for medical record technicians started up in hospital schools and junior colleges.

In recent years the computerization of records, the growing importance of privacy and freedom of information issues, and the changing requirements of insurance carriers have all had major impacts on the field of medical records technology. These areas will undoubtedly continue to reshape the field in future years.

THE JOB

A patient's medical record consists of all relevant information and observations of any health care workers who have dealt with the patient. It may contain, for example, several diagnoses, X-ray and laboratory reports, electrocardiogram tracings, test results, and drugs prescribed. This summary of the patient's medical history is very important to the physician in making speedy and correct decisions about care. Later, information from the record is often needed when authenticating legal forms and insurance claims. The medical record documents the adequacy and appropriateness of the care received by the patient and is the basis of any investigation when the care is questioned in any way.

Patterns and trends can be traced when data from many records are considered together. These types of statistical reports are used by many different groups. Hospital administrators, scientists, public health agencies, accrediting and licensing bodies, people who evaluate the effectiveness of current programs or plan future ones, and medical reimbursement organizations are examples of some groups that rely on health care statistics. Medical records can provide the data to show whether a new treatment or medication really works, the relative effectiveness of alternative treatments or medications, or patterns that yield clues about the causes or methods of preventing certain kinds of disease.

Medical record technicians routinely prepare, handle, and safeguard individual records and the statistical information extracted from groups of records. Their specific tasks and the scope of their responsibilities depend a great deal on the size and type of the employing institution. In large organizations there may be a number of technicians and other employees working with medical records. The technicians may serve as assistants to the medical record administrator as needed or may regularly specialize in some particular phase of the work done by the department. In small facilities, however, technicians often carry out the whole range of activities and may function fairly independently, perhaps bearing the full responsibility for all day-to-day operations of the department. A technician in a small facility may even be a department director. Sometimes technicians handle medical records and also spend part of their time helping out in the business or admitting office.

Whether they work in hospitals or other settings, medical record technicians must organize, transfer, analyze, preserve, and locate vast quantities of detailed information when needed. The sources of this information include physicians, nurses, laboratory workers, and other members of the health care team.

In a hospital, a patient's cumulative record goes to the medical record department at the end of the hospital stay. A technician checks over the information in the file to be sure that all the essential reports and data are included and appear accurate. Certain specific items must be supplied in any record, such as signatures, dates, the patient's physical and social history, the results of physical examinations, provisional and final diagnoses, periodic progress notes on the patient's condition during the hospital stay, medications prescribed and administered, therapeutic treatments, surgical procedures, and an assessment of the outcome or the condition at the time of discharge. If any item is missing, the technician sends the record to the person who is responsible for supplying the information. After all necessary information has been received and the record has passed the review, it is considered the official document describing the patient's case.

The record is then passed to a *medical record coder*. Coders are responsible for assigning a numeric code to every diagnosis and procedure listed in a patient's file. Most hospitals in the United States use a nationally accepted system for coding. The lists of diseases, procedures, and conditions are published in classification manuals that medical records personnel refer to frequently. By reducing information in different forms to a single consistent coding system, the data contained in the record is rendered much easier to handle, tabulate, and analyze. It can be indexed under any suitable heading, such as by patient, disease, type of surgery, physician attending the case, and so forth. Cross-indexing is likely to be an important part of the medical record technician's job. Because the same coding systems are used nearly everywhere in the United States, the data may be used not only by people working inside the hospital, but may also be submitted to one of the various programs that pool information obtained from many institutions.

After the information on the medical record has been coded, technicians may use a packaged computer program to assign the patient to one of several hundred diagnosis-related groupings, or DRGs. The DRG for the patient's stay determines the amount of money the hospital will receive if the patient is covered by Medicare or one of the other insurance programs that base their reimbursement on DRGs.

Because information in medical records is used to determine how much hospitals are paid for caring for patients, the accuracy of the work done by medical records personnel is vital. A coding error could cause the hospital or patient to lose money.

Another vital part of the job concerns filing. Regardless of how accurately and completely information is gathered and stored, it is worthless unless it can be retrieved promptly. If paper records are kept, technicians are usually responsible for preparing records for storage, filing them, and getting them out of storage when needed. In some organizations technicians supervise other personnel who carry out these tasks.

In many health care facilities computers, rather than paper, are used for nearly all the medical record keeping. In such cases, medical and nursing staff make notes on an electronic chart. They enter patient-care information into computer files, and medical record technicians access the information using their own terminals. Computers have greatly simplified many traditional routine tasks of the medical records department, such as generating daily hospital census figures, tabulating data for research purposes, and updating special registries of certain types of health problems, such as cancer and stroke.

In the past some medical records that were originally on paper were later photographed and stored on microfilm, particularly after they were a year or two old. Medical record technicians may be responsible for retrieving and maintaining those films. It is not unusual for a health care institution to have a combination of paper and microfilm files as well as computerized record storage, reflecting the evolution of technology for storing information.

Confidentiality and privacy laws have a major bearing on the medical records field. The laws vary in different states for different types of data, but in all cases, maintaining the confidentiality of individual records is of major concern to medical records workers. All individual records must be in secure storage but also be available for retrieval and specified kinds of properly authorized use. Technicians may be responsible for retrieving and releasing this information. They may prepare records to be released in response to a patient's written authorization, a subpoena, or a court order. This requires special knowledge of legal statutes and often requires consultation with attorneys, judges, insurance agents, and other parties with legitimate rights to access information about a person's health and medical treatment.

Medical record technicians may participate in the quality assurance, risk management, and utilization review activities of a health care facility. In these cases they may serve as *data abstractors* and *data analysts,* reviewing records against established standards to ensure quality of care. They may also prepare statistical reports for the medical or administrative staff that reviews appropriateness of care.

With more specialized training, medical record technicians may participate in medical research activities by maintaining special records, called registries, related to such areas as cancer, heart disease, transplants, or adverse outcomes of pregnancies. In some cases they are required to abstract and code information from records of patients with certain medical conditions. These technicians also may prepare statistical reports and trend analyses for the use of medical researchers.

REQUIREMENTS

High School

If you are contemplating a career in medical records, you should take as many high school English classes as possible, because technicians need both written and verbal communication skills to prepare reports and communicate with other health care personnel. Basic math or business math is very desirable because statistical skills are important in some job functions. Biology courses will help to familiarize yourself with the terminology that medical record technicians use. Other science courses, computer training, typing proficiency, and experience with office procedures are also helpful.

Postsecondary Training

Most employers prefer to hire medical record technicians who have completed a two-year associate's degree program accredited by the American Medical Association's Commission on Accreditation for Health Informatics and Information Management Education and the American Health Information Management Association (AHIMA). There are approximately 245 of these accredited programs available throughout the United States, mostly offered in junior and community colleges. They usually include classroom instruction in such subjects as anatomy, physiology, medical terminology, medical record science, word processing, medical aspects of record keeping, statistics, computers in health care, personnel supervision, business management, English, and office skills.

In addition to classroom instruction, the student is given supervised clinical experience in the medical records departments of local health care facilities. This provides students with practical experience in performing many of the functions learned in the classroom and the opportunity to interact with health care professionals.

Certification or Licensing

Medical record technicians who have completed an accredited training program are eligible to take a national qualifying examination to earn the credential of registered health information technician (RHIT). Most health care institutions prefer to hire individuals with an RHIT credential, as it signifies that they have met the standards established by the AHIMA as the mark of a qualified health professional. AHIMA also offers certification to medical coders and health information administrators. Specialized certifications in medical coding are also available from the American Academy of Professional Coders.

Other Requirements

Medical records are extremely detailed and precise. Sloppy work could have serious consequences in terms of payment to the hospital or physician, validity of the patient records for later use, and validity of research based on data from medical records. Therefore, a prospective technician must have the capacity to do consistently reliable and accurate routine work. Records must be completed and maintained with care and attention to detail. You may be the only person who checks the entire record, and you must understand the responsibility that accompanies this task.

The technician needs to be able to work rapidly as well as accurately. In many medical record departments, the workload is very heavy, and you must be well organized and efficient in order to stay on top of the job. You must be able to complete your work accurately, in spite of interruptions, such as phone calls and requests for assistance. You also need to be discreet, as you will deal with records that are private and sometimes sensitive.

Computer skills also are essential, and some experience in transcribing dictated reports may be useful.

EXPLORING

To learn more about this and other medical careers, you may be able to find summer, part-time, or volunteer work in a hospital or other health care facility. Sometimes such jobs are available in the medical records area of an organization. You may also be able to arrange to talk with someone working as a medical record technician or administrator. Faculty and counselors at schools that offer medical record technician training programs may also be good sources of information. You also can learn more about this profession by reading journals and other literature available at a public library.

EMPLOYERS

Although two out of five of the 170,000 medical record technicians employed in the United States work in hospitals, many work in other health care settings, including health maintenance organizations (HMOs), industrial clinics, skilled nursing facilities, rehabilitation centers, large group medical practices, ambulatory care centers, and state and local government health agencies. Technicians also work for computer firms, consulting firms, and government agencies. Records are maintained in all these facilities, although record-keeping procedures vary.

Not all medical record technicians are employed in a single health care facility; some serve as consultants to several small facilities. Other technicians do not work in health care settings at all. They may be employed by health and property liability insurance companies to collect and review information on medical claims. A few are self-employed, providing medical transcription services.

STARTING OUT

Most successful medical record technicians are graduates of two-year accredited programs. Graduates of these programs should check with their schools' career services offices for job leads. Those who have taken the accrediting exam and have become certified can use the AHIMA's resume referral service.

You may also apply directly to the personnel departments of hospitals, nursing homes, outpatient clinics, and surgery centers. Many job openings are also listed in the classified sections of local newspapers and with private and public employment agencies.

ADVANCEMENT

Medical record technicians may be able to achieve some advancement and salary increase without additional training simply by taking on greater responsibility in their job function. With experience, technicians may move to supervisory or department head positions, depending on the type and structure of the employing organization. Another means of advancing is through specialization in a certain area of the job. Some technicians specialize in coding, particularly Medicare coding or tumor registry. With a broad range of experience, a medical record technician may be able to become an independent consultant. Generally, technicians with an associate's degree and the RHIT designation are most likely to advance.

More assured job advancement and salary increase come with the completion of a bachelor's degree in medical record administration. The bachelor's degree, along with AHIMA accreditation, makes the technician eligible for a supervisory position, such as department director. Because of a general shortage of medical record administrators, hospitals often assist technicians who are working toward a bachelor's degree by providing flexible scheduling and financial aid or tuition reimbursement.

EARNINGS

The salaries of medical record technicians are greatly influenced by the location, size, and type of employing institution, as well as the technician's training and experience. According to the AHIMA, beginning technicians with an associate's degree can earn between $20,000 to $30,000 annually. Those who have earned a bachelor's degree can expect to earn between $30,000 and $50,000 a year. With five years of experience, technicians can earn up to $75,000 annually.

According to the U.S. Department of Labor, the median annual earnings of medical record and health information technicians were $29,290 in 2007. Salaries ranged from less than $19,690 to more than $47,440.

In general, medical record technicians working in large urban hospitals make the most money, and those in rural areas make the least. Like most hospital employees, medical record technicians usually receive paid vacations and holidays, life and health insurance, and retirement benefits.

WORK ENVIRONMENT

Medical records departments are usually pleasant, clean, well lit, and air-conditioned. Sometimes, however, paper or microfilm records are kept in cramped, out-of-the-way quarters. Although the work requires thorough and careful attention to detail, there may be a constant bustle of activity in the technician's work area, which can be disruptive. The job is likely to involve frequent routine contact with nurses, physicians, hospital administrators, other health care professionals, attorneys, and insurance agents. On occasion, individuals with whom the technicians may interact are demanding or difficult. In such cases technicians may find that the job carries a high level of frustration.

A 40-hour workweek is the norm, but because hospitals operate on a 24-hour basis, the job may regularly include night or weekend hours. Part-time work is sometimes available.

The work is extremely detailed and may be tedious. Some technicians spend the majority of their day sitting at a desk, working on a computer. Others may spend hours filing paper records or retrieving them from storage.

In many hospital settings, the medical record technician experiences pressure caused by a heavy workload. As the demands for health care cost containment and productivity increase, medical record technicians may be required to produce a significantly greater volume of high-quality work in shorter periods of time.

Nonetheless, the knowledge that their work is significant for patients and medical research can be personally very satisfying for medical record technicians.

OUTLOOK

Employment prospects through 2016 are very good. The U.S. Department of Labor predicts that employment in this field will grow faster than the average for all careers. The demand for well-trained medical record technicians will grow rapidly and will continue to exceed the supply. This expectation is related to the health care needs of a population that is both growing and aging and the trend toward more technologically sophisticated medicine and greater use of diagnostic procedures. It is also related to the increased requirements of regulatory bodies that scrutinize both costs and quality of care of health care providers. Because of the fear of medical malpractice lawsuits, doctors and other health care providers are documenting their diagnoses and treatments in greater detail. Also, because of the high cost of health care, insurance companies, government agencies, and courts are examining medical records with a more critical eye. These factors combine to ensure a healthy job outlook for medical record technicians.

Opportunities will be best in offices of physicians, particularly in large group practices, nursing and residential care facilities, home health care services, and outpatient care centers.

Technicians with associate's degrees and RHIT status will have the best prospects, and the importance of such qualifications is likely to increase.

FOR MORE INFORMATION

For information on training and certification, contact
American Academy of Professional Coders
2480 South 3850 West, Suite B
Salt Lake City, UT 84120-7208
Tel: 800-626-2633
Email: info@aapc.com
http://www.aapc.com

For information on earnings, careers in health information management, and accredited programs, contact
American Health Information Management Association
233 North Michigan Avenue, 21st Floor
Chicago, IL 60601-5809
Tel: 312-233-1100
Email: info@ahima.org
http://www.ahima.org

For a list of schools offering accredited programs in health information management, contact
Commission on Accreditation for Health Informatics and Information Management Education
233 North Michigan Avenue, 21st Floor
Chicago, IL 60601-5800
http://www.cahiim.org

For information on a career as a cancer registrar, contact
National Cancer Registrars Association
1340 Braddock Place, Suite 203
Alexandria, VA 22314-1651
Tel: 703-299-6640
http://www.ncra-usa.org

Medical Secretaries

QUICK FACTS

School Subjects
English
Health
Speech

Personal Skills
Communication/ideas
Following instructions

Work Environment
Primarily indoors
Primarily one location

Minimum Education Level
High school diploma

Salary Range
$20,260 to $28,950 to
$41,860+

Certification or Licensing
Voluntary

Outlook
Faster than the average

DOT
201

GOE
09.02.02

NOC
1243

O*NET-SOC
43-6013.00

OVERVIEW

Medical secretaries perform administrative and clerical work in medical offices, hospitals, or private physicians' offices. They answer phone calls, order supplies, handle correspondence, bill patients, complete insurance forms, and transcribe dictation. Medical secretaries also handle bookkeeping, greet patients, schedule appointments, arrange hospital admissions, and schedule surgeries. There are approximately 408,000 medical secretaries employed throughout the United States.

HISTORY

During the industrial expansion at the turn of the 20th century, businesses faced a paperwork crisis. Secretaries helped to solve this problem by using technologies such as adding machines, telephones, and typewriters. At the time, many people aspired to be secretaries. In the 1930s the number of male secretaries dwindled, and women began to dominate this segment of the office workforce.

In the modern office, secretaries, also known as *administrative assistants, office coordinators, executive assistants,* and *office managers,* use computers, the Internet, and other equipment to perform vital information management functions.

As insurance and billing practices in the health care industry have grown complicated, and physicians have begun to see more patients, the career of medical secretary has emerged to handle administrative responsibilities that were previously taken care of by physicians, nurses, and other health care professionals. Today, medical secretaries are key players in keeping medical facilities operating at top efficiency.

Learn More About It

Green, Stephanie, and Pauline Young. *The Essential Medical Secretary: Foundations for Good Practice.* 2d ed. New York: Bailliere Tindall, 2004.
Humphrey, Doris. *Contemporary Medical Office Procedures.* 3d ed. Florence, Ky.: Delmar Cengage Learning, 2003.
Morimoto, Valeri, S. *A Handbook for Medical Assistants and Medical Secretaries.* Montgomery, Ala.: E-BookTime, LLC, 2005.

THE JOB

Medical secretaries play important roles in the health care profession. They transcribe dictation, prepare correspondence, and assist physicians or medical scientists with reports, speeches, articles, and conference proceedings. Medical secretaries also record simple medical histories, arrange for patients to be hospitalized, and order supplies. Most need to be familiar with insurance rules, billing practices, and hospital or laboratory procedures.

Doctors rely on medical secretaries to keep administrative operations under control. Secretaries are the information clearinghouses for the office. They schedule appointments, handle phone calls, organize and maintain paper and electronic files, and produce correspondence for the office. Medical secretaries must have basic technical skills to operate office equipment such as fax machines, photocopiers, and switchboard systems. Increasingly, they use computers to run spreadsheet, word processing, database, or desktop publishing programs.

REQUIREMENTS

High School

Most employers require medical secretaries to have a high school diploma and be able to type between 60 and 90 words per minute. In order to handle more specialized duties, you must be familiar with medical terms and procedures and be able to use medical software programs. In addition, you need to have basic math skills and strong written and verbal communication skills to write up correspondence and handle patient inquiries. English, speech, and health classes will help you prepare for this career.

Postsecondary Training

One- and two-year programs are offered by many vocational, community, and business schools covering the skills needed for secretarial work. For more specialized training, some schools offer medical secretarial programs, covering the basics such as typing, filing, and accounting, as well as more specialized courses on medical stenography, first aid, medical terminology, and medical office procedures.

Certification or Licensing

Certification is not required for a job as a medical secretary, but obtaining it may bring increased opportunities, earnings, and responsibility. The International Association of Administrative Professionals offers the certified professional secretary (CPS) and certified administrative professional (CAP) designations. To achieve CPS or CAP certification, you must meet certain experience requirements and pass a rigorous exam covering a number of general secretarial topics.

Other Requirements

To succeed as a medical secretary, you must be trustworthy and use discretion when dealing with confidential medical records. You must also have a pleasant and confident personality for handling the public and a desire to help others in a dependable and conscientious manner.

EXPLORING

The best way to learn about this career is to speak with an experienced medical secretary about his or her work. Ask your school guidance counselor to set up an information interview with a medical secretary or to arrange a tour of a medical facility so you can see secretaries in action.

EMPLOYERS

Approximately 408,000 medical secretaries are employed in the United States. Medical secretaries work in private physicians' offices, hospitals, outpatient clinics, emergency care facilities, research laboratories, and large health organizations, such as the Mayo Medical Clinic. The Mayo Clinic branches, located in Florida, Massachusetts, Minnesota, and Arizona, employ more than 1,000 medical secretaries who work for nearly 1,200 physicians and scientists. A majority of medical secretaries work with one or two physicians practicing in a clinical outpatient care setting. The remainder provide support to physicians and scientists in clinical and research laboratories, hospitals, or Mayo Clinic's medical school.

STARTING OUT

To find work in this field, you should apply directly to hospitals, clinics, and physicians' offices. Potential positions might be listed with school or college career services offices or in newspaper want ads. Networking with medical secretaries is another inside track to job leads, because employers tend to trust employee recommendations.

ADVANCEMENT

Promotions for secretaries who work in doctors' offices are usually limited to increases in salary and responsibilities. Medical secretaries employed by clinics or hospitals can advance to executive positions, such as senior secretary, clerical supervisor, or office manager; or into more administrative jobs, such as medical records clerk, administrative assistant, or unit manager.

EARNINGS

The U.S. Department of Labor reports that medical secretaries earned a median annual salary of $28,950 in 2007. Salaries ranged from less than $20,260 to more than $41,860. The mean salary in 2007 for medical secretaries employed in physicians' offices was $29,350; in hospitals, $29,530; and in dentist offices, $34,430.

Most employers offer vacation, sick leave, and medical benefits. Many also provide life, dental, and vision care insurance; retirement benefits; and profit sharing.

WORK ENVIRONMENT

Medical secretaries usually work 40 hours a week, Monday through Friday, during regular business hours. However, some work extended hours one or two days a week, depending on the physician's office hours. They do their work in well-lit, pleasant surroundings, but could encounter stressful emergency situations.

OUTLOOK

While the demand for secretaries in the general sector is expected to grow as fast as the average for all occupations, the U.S. Department of Labor projects a higher demand for medical secretaries, expecting the occupation to grow faster than the average for all occupations through 2016.

Health services are demanding more from their support personnel, and salary levels are increasing accordingly. Technological advances enable secretaries to be more productive and able to handle the duties once done by managers or other staff. The distribution of work has shifted; secretaries receive fewer requests for typing and filing jobs. Instead, they do more technical work requiring computer skills beyond keyboarding. The job outlook appears brightest for those who are up to date on the latest programs and technological advances.

FOR MORE INFORMATION

For information on professional certification, contact
International Association of Administrative Professionals
PO Box 20404
Kansas City, MO 64195-0404
Tel: 816-891-6600
Email: service@iaap-hq.org
http://www.iaap-hq.org

The Mayo Clinic is a major employer of medical secretaries. Visit its Web site for more information.
Mayo Clinic
http://www.mayoclinic.org/jobs

Medical Transcriptionists

OVERVIEW

Doctors and other health care professionals often make recordings documenting what happened during their patients' appointments or surgical procedures. *Medical transcriptionists* listen to these recordings and transcribe, or type, reports of what the doctor said. The reports are then included in patients' charts. Medical transcriptionists work in a variety of health care settings, including hospitals, clinics, and doctors' offices, as well as for transcription companies or out of their own homes. There are about 98,000 medical transcriptionists working in the United States. Medical transcriptionists are also called *medical transcribers, medical stenographers,* or *medical language specialists.*

HISTORY

Health care documentation dates back to the beginnings of medical treatment. Doctors used to keep their own handwritten records of a patient's medical history and treatment. After 1900, medical stenographers took on this role. Stenographers worked alongside doctors, writing down doctors' reports in shorthand. This changed with the invention of the dictating machine, which led to the development of the career of medical transcription.

The first commercial dictating machine, using a wax cylinder record, was produced in 1887. It was based on Thomas A. Edison's phonograph, invented in 1877. Technology has come a long way since then. Recent advances in the field include Internet transcription

A Portrait of Medical Transcriptionists, 2007

- Nearly 45 percent of medical transcriptionists were age 50 and over—which suggests that opportunities for aspiring transcriptionists will be good in coming years as many existing workers reach retirement age.
- Nearly 96 percent of medical transcriptionists were women.
- 48.8 percent of medical transcriptionists had an associate's degree or higher.
- 53 percent of medical transcriptionists had graduated from a medical transcription education/training program.

Source: Bentley College Study of Healthcare Documentation Production/Association for Healthcare Documentation Integrity

capabilities and voice- (or speech-) recognition software. The latter electronically transcribes recorded spoken word, which means that a medical transcriptionist does not have to type out all the dictation. Given the complexity of medical terminology, however, voice recognition programs are likely to make mistakes, so there is still plenty of work for the medical transcriptionist, who must carefully proofread the report to catch and correct any errors.

THE JOB

Medical transcriptionists transcribe (type into printed format) a dictated (oral) report recorded by a doctor or another health care professional. They work for primary care physicians as well as health care professionals in various medical specialties, including cardiology, immunology, oncology, podiatry, radiology, and urology. The medical transcriptionist usually types up the report while listening to the recording through a transcriber machine's headset, using a foot pedal to stop or rewind the recording as necessary. Some doctors dictate over the telephone, and others use the Internet.

The report consists of information gathered during a patient's office appointment or hospital visit and covers the patient's medical history and treatment. Doctors dictate information about patient consultations, physical examinations, results from laboratory work or X rays, medical tests, psychiatric evaluations, patient diagnosis and prognosis, surgical procedures, a patient's hospital stay and discharge, autopsies, and so on. Often doctors will use abbreviations while dictating. The medical transcriptionist must type out the full names of those abbreviations.

Because the report becomes a permanent part of a patient's medical record and is referred to by the same doctor or other members of the patient's health care team during future office visits or when determining future medical treatment, it must be accurate. This includes dates and the spelling of medications, procedures, diseases, medical instruments and supplies, and laboratory values.

Medical transcriptionists review reports and make corrections to grammar, punctuation, and spelling. They read for clarity, consistentcy, and completeness. Because these kinds of corrections are expected, the final report does not need to be identical to the original dictation in those respects.

Being a medical transcriptionist is not all about typing and proofreading. Medical transcriptionists are very familiar with medical terminology. When recording their reports, doctors use medical terms that are relevant to a patient's condition and treatment. Such terms might be names of diseases or medications. Medical transcriptionists understand what these medical terms mean and how they are spelled. They understand enough about various diseases and their symptoms, treatments, and prognoses as to be able to figure out what a doctor is saying if the recording is a little garbled. They have a good understanding of medicine and know about human anatomy and physiology. If what the doctor says on the tape is unclear, a medical transcriptionist often has to determine the appropriate word or words based on the context. However, medical transcriptionists never guess when it comes to medications, conditions, medical history, and treatments. A patient could receive improper and even damaging treatment if a diagnosis is made based on a report containing errors. Medical transcriptionists contact the doctor if they are uncertain or they leave a blank in the report, depending on the employer's or client's expectations and guidelines. After the medical transcriptionist reviews the report, it is given to the doctor, who also reviews it and then signs it if it is acceptable—or returns it to the transcriptionist for correction, if necessary. Once it has been signed, the report is placed in the patient's permanent medical file.

Many medical transcriptionists use voice recognition software to create documents electronically from oral dictation, eliminating much of their typing work. Medical transcriptionists still have to review the transcription for accuracy and format.

While some transcriptionists only do transcribing, other transcriptionists, often those who work in doctors' offices or clinics, may have additional responsibilities. They may deal with patients, answer the phone, handle the mail, and perform other clerical tasks. And transcriptionists may be asked to file or deliver the reports to other doctors, lawyers, or other people who request them.

A growing number of medical transcriptionists work out of their homes, either telecommuting as employees or subcontractors or as self-employed workers. As technology becomes more sophisticated, this trend is likely to continue. Medical transcriptionists who work out of their homes have some degree of mobility and can live where they choose, taking their jobs with them. These workers must keep up to date with their medical resources and equipment. Because terminology continues to change, medical transcriptionists regularly buy revised editions of some of the standard medical resources.

REQUIREMENTS

High School

English and grammar classes are important in preparing to become a medical transcriptionist. Focus on becoming an excellent speller. If you understand the meanings of word prefixes and suffixes (many of which come from Greek and Latin), it will be easier for you to learn medical terminology, since many terms are formed by adding a prefix and/or a suffix to a word or root. If your high school offers Greek or Latin classes, take one; otherwise, try to take Greek or Latin when you continue your studies after high school.

Biology and health classes will give you a solid introduction to the human body and how it functions, preparing you to take more advanced classes in anatomy and physiology after you graduate. Be sure to learn how to type by taking a class or teaching yourself. Practice typing regularly to build up your speed and accuracy. Word processing and computer classes are also useful.

Postsecondary Training

Some junior, community, and business colleges and vocational schools have medical transcription programs. You can also learn the business of medical transcription by taking a correspondence course. To be accepted into a medical transcription program, you might need to have a minimum typing speed. The Association for Healthcare Documentation Integrity (AHDI) recommends that medical transcriptionists complete a nine- to 18-month program offering an associate's degree, but this is not necessary for you to find a job.

You should take courses in English grammar as well as medical terminology, anatomy, physiology, and pharmacology. Some of the more specific classes you might take include medicolegal concepts and ethics, human disease and pathophysiology, health care records management, and medical grammar and editing. Certain programs offer on-the-job training, which will help when you are looking for full-time employment.

The AHDI has a mentoring program for students who are studying medical transcription. Students can make important contacts in the field and learn much from experienced professionals.

Certification or Licensing
Voluntary certification for medical transcriptionists is available from the AHDI. The registered medical transcriptionist designation is available to applicants who are recent graduates of medical transcription education programs who have fewer than two years experience in acute care and pass an examination. The certified medical transcriptionist designation is awarded to applicants with at least two years of acute care transcription experience and who pass an examination. The fellow designation is awarded to medical transcriptionists who have "achieved a balance of successful activities in their profession that goes beyond regular transcription practice."

While medical transcriptionists do not need to be certified to find a job, it is highly recommended as a sign of achievement and professionalism. Certified transcriptionists will probably more readily find employment and earn higher salaries.

Other Requirements
A love of language and grammar is an important quality, and accuracy and attention to detail are absolute musts for a medical transcriptionist. It is essential that you correctly type up information as spoken on the recording. You must be able to sift through background sounds on the recording and accurately record what the medical professional says. Doctors dictate at the same time they are with a patient or later from their office or maybe even as they go about their daily routine, perhaps while eating, driving in traffic, or walking along a busy street. In each of these cases, the recording will likely include noises or conversations that at times drown out or make unclear what the doctor is saying.

Many doctors grew up outside of the United States and do not speak English as their first language, so they may not have a thorough understanding of English or they may speak with an accent. You must have a good ear to be able to decipher what these doctors are saying.

In addition to having accurate typing skills, you will also need to type quickly if you want to make higher wages and get more clients. A solid understanding of word processing software will help you to be more productive. An example of this is the use of macros, or keystroke combinations that are used for repetitive actions, such as typing the same long, hard-to-spell word or phrase time and again.

If you suffer from repetitive strain injuries, then this would not be a suitable profession.

Flexibility is also important because you must be able to adapt to the different skills and needs of various health care professionals.

Medical transcriptionists should be able to concentrate and be prepared to sit in one place for long periods at a time, either typing or reading. For this reason, it is important that you take regular breaks. An ability to work independently will help you whether you are self-employed or have an office position, since you do most of your work sitting at a computer.

Medical transcriptionists are required to keep patient records confidential, just as doctors are, so integrity and discretion are important.

EXPLORING

There is plenty of accessible reading material aimed at medical transcriptionists. This is a good way to learn more about the field and decide if it sounds interesting to you. Several of the Web sites listed at the end of this article feature self-assessment tests and articles about medical transcription. Marylou Bunting, a home-based certified medical transcriptionist, recommends that you get a medical dictionary and *Physicians' Desk Reference* to familiarize yourself with terminology. See if your local library has *Health Data Matrix* and browse through some issues. The Internet is a great resource for would-be medical transcriptionists. Find a bulletin board or mailing list and talk to professionals in the field, perhaps conducting an information interview.

Bunting also suggests that you "put yourself in a medical setting as soon and as often as you can." Ask if your doctor can use your help in any way or apply for a volunteer position at a local hospital. Ask to be assigned to the hospital's medical records department, which won't give you the opportunity to transcribe, but will give you some experience dealing with medical records.

EMPLOYERS

There are approximately 98,000 medical transcriptionists working in the United States. About 41 percent work in hospitals and 29 percent work in doctors' offices and clinics. Others work for laboratories, medical centers, colleges and universities, medical libraries, insurance companies, transcription companies, rehabilitation centers, temp agencies, and even veterinary facilities. Medical transcriptionists can also find government jobs, with public health or veterans hospitals.

STARTING OUT

It can be difficult to get started in this field, especially if you do not have any work experience. Some medical transcriptionists start out working as administrative assistants or receptionists in doctors' offices. They become acquainted with medical terminology and office procedures, and they make important contacts in the medical profession. According to the AHDI, a smaller doctor's office may be more apt to hire an inexperienced medical transcriptionist than a hospital or transcription service would be.

Marylou Bunting recommends that you try to get an apprenticeship position since on-the-job experience seems to be a prerequisite for most jobs. (Visit http://www.ahdionline.org/scriptcontent/apprentice. cfm for more information on approved apprenticeship programs.) Or perhaps you can find an internship with a transcription company. Once you have some experience, you can look for another position through classified ads, job search agencies, or Internet resources. You can also find job leads through word-of-mouth and professional contacts. The AHDI's Web site features job postings, and the organization itself is an invaluable resource for the medical transcriptionist. Local chapters hold periodic meetings, which is a good way to network with other professionals in the field.

ADVANCEMENT

There are few actual advancement opportunities for medical transcriptionists. Those who become faster and more accurate will have an easier time securing better-paying positions or lining up new clients. Skilled and experienced medical transcriptionists can become supervisors of transcription departments or managers of transcription companies, or they might even form their own transcription companies. Some also become teachers, consultants, or authors or editors of books on the subject of medical transcription.

EARNINGS

Medical transcriptionists are paid in a variety of ways, depending on the employer or client. Payment might be made based on the number of hours worked or the number of lines transcribed. Monetary incentives might be offered to hourly transcriptionists achieving a high rate of production.

The U.S. Department of Labor reports that in 2007 the lowest paid 10 percent of all medical transcriptionists made less than $22,160, and the highest paid 10 percent made more than $44,070. Medical transcriptionists who worked in medical and diagnostic laboratories earned a mean salary of $36,640 in 2007. Those employed in hospitals earned $32,630, and those who worked in offices and clinics of medical doctors earned $31,250 in 2007. Medical transcriptionists who are certified earn higher average salaries than transcriptionists who have not earned certification.

Medical transcriptionists working in a hospital or company setting can expect to receive the usual benefits, including paid vacation, sick days, and health insurance. Tuition reimbursement and 401(k) plans may also be offered. Home-based medical transcriptionists who are employed by a company may be entitled to the same benefits that in-house staff members receive. It is important to check with each individual company to be sure. Self-employed medical transcriptionists have to make arrangements for their own health and retirement plans and other benefits.

WORK ENVIRONMENT

Most medical transcriptionists work in an office setting, either at their employer's place of business or in their own homes. They generally sit at desks in front of computers and have transcribers or dictation machines and medical reference books at hand. Home-based workers and sometimes even office workers must invest a substantial amount of money for reference books and equipment on an ongoing basis, to keep up with changes in medical terminology and technology.

Transcriptionists who are not self-employed usually put in a 40-hour week. Some medical transcriptionists working in hospitals are assigned to the second or third shift. Independent contractors, on the other hand, clock their hours when they have work to do. Sometimes this will be part-time or on the weekends or at night. If they are busy enough, some work more hours than in the normal workweek.

Because medical transcriptionists spend such a long time typing at a computer, the risk of repetitive stress injuries is present. Other physical problems may also occur, including eyestrain from staring at a computer screen and back or neck pain from sitting in one position for long periods at a time.

OUTLOOK

The U.S. Department of Labor reports that employment of medical transcriptionists is expected to grow faster than the average for all careers through 2016. An aging and growing population, a continuing need for electronic documentation that can easily be shared among health care professionals, and the ongoing need for transcriptionists to edit patients' records, edit documents generated by speech recognition systems, and find errors in medical reports will create excellent opportunities for workers in the field. Opportunities will be best for medical transcriptionists who are certified.

Although employment opportunities are expected to continue to be steady in hospitals, the fastest job growth is expected for transcriptionists who work in offices of physicians, especially large group practices.

FOR MORE INFORMATION

This publication contains an assortment of articles of interest to health information management professionals, including medical transcriptionists.
Advance for Health Information Professionals
http://health-information.advanceweb.com

This professional organization for medical transcriptionists provides many online resources, including suggestions on how to prepare for a career in medical transcription, a career overview, tips for students, and tips for those interested in becoming self-employed medical transcriptionists.
Association for Healthcare Documentation Integrity
4230 Kiernan Avenue, Suite 130
Modesto, CA 95356-9322
Tel: 800-982-2182
Email: ahdi@ahdionline.org
http://www.ahdionline.org

For an overview of the job, several language resources and tests, and sample reports, visit
Medword—Medical Transcription
http://www.medword.com

This networking resource for professionals includes discussion forums and interviews.
MT Daily
http://www.mtdaily.com

Visit this Web site for an extensive glossary, a huge list of "stumper terms" for medical transcriptionists, links to other medical-related

dictionaries and resources, sample operative reports, book sugges-
tions, chat forums, and classified ads.
    MT Desk
    http://www.mtdesk.com

This site features preparatory materials, including quizzes, proof-
reading tests, and crossword puzzles; articles about getting started;
tips on transcribing, punctuation, and grammar; and listings of rec-
ommended resources.
    MT Monthly and Review of Systems School of Medical Tran-
    scription
    http://www.mtmonthly.com

Office Clerks

OVERVIEW

Office clerks perform a variety of clerical tasks that help an office run smoothly, including file maintenance, mail sorting, and record keeping. In large companies, office clerks might have specialized tasks such as inputting data into a computer, but in most cases, clerks are flexible and have many duties, including typing, answering telephones, taking messages, responding to emails, making photocopies, and preparing mailings. Office clerks usually work under close supervision, often with experienced clerks directing their activities. There are approximately 3.2 million office clerks employed in the United States.

HISTORY

Before the 18th century many businesspeople did their own office work, such as shipping products, accepting payments, and recording inventory. The industrial revolution changed the nature of business by popularizing the specialization of labor, which allowed companies to increase their output dramatically. At this time office clerks were brought in to handle the growing amount of clerical duties.

Office workers have become more important as computers, word processors, and other technological advances have increased both the volume of business information available and the speed with which administrative decisions can be made. The number of office workers in the United States has grown as more trained personnel are needed to handle the volume of business communication and information. Businesses and government agencies depend on skilled office workers to file and sort documents,

QUICK FACTS

School Subjects
Business
English
Mathematics

Personal Skills
Communication/ideas
Following instructions

Work Environment
Primarily indoors
Primarily one location

Minimum Education Level
High school diploma

Salary Range
$15,490 to $24,460 to $38,780+

Certification or Licensing
Voluntary

Outlook
About as fast as the average

DOT
209

GOE
09.07.02

NOC
1411

O*NET-SOC
43-9061.00

operate office equipment, and cooperate with others to ensure the flow of information.

THE JOB

Office clerks usually perform a variety of tasks as part of their overall job responsibility. They may type or file bills, statements, and business correspondence. They may stuff envelopes, answer telephones, respond to emails, and sort mail. Office clerks also enter data into computers, run errands, and operate office equipment such as photocopiers, fax machines, and switchboards. In the course of an average day, an office clerk usually performs a combination of these and other clerical tasks, spending an hour or so on one task and then moving on to another as directed by an office manager or other supervisor.

An office clerk may work with other office personnel, such as a bookkeeper or accountant, to maintain a company's financial records. The clerk may type and mail invoices and sort payments as they come in, keep payroll records, or take inventories. With more experience, the clerk may be asked to update customer files to reflect receipt of payments and verify records for accuracy.

Office clerks often deliver messages from one office worker to another, an especially important responsibility in larger companies. Clerks may relay questions and answers from one department head to another. Similarly, clerks may relay messages from people outside the company or employees who are outside of the office to those working in house. Office clerks may also work with other personnel on individual projects, such as preparing a yearly budget or making sure a mass mailing gets out on time.

Administrative clerks assist in the efficient operation of an office by compiling business records; providing information to sales personnel and customers; and preparing and sending out bills, policies, invoices, and other business correspondence. Administrative clerks may also keep financial records and prepare the payroll. *File clerks* review and classify letters, documents, articles, and other information and then file this material so it can be quickly retrieved at a later time. They contribute to the smooth distribution of information at a company.

Some clerks have titles that describe where they work and the jobs they do. For example, *congressional-district aides* work for the elected officials of their U.S. congressional district. *Police clerks* handle routine office procedures in police stations, and *concrete products dispatchers* work with construction firms on building projects.

REQUIREMENTS

High School

To prepare for a career as an office clerk, you should take courses in English, mathematics, and as many business-related subjects, such as keyboarding and bookkeeping, as possible. Community colleges and vocational schools often offer business education courses that provide training for general office workers.

Postsecondary Training

A high school diploma is usually sufficient for beginning office clerks, although business courses covering office machine operation and bookkeeping are also helpful. To succeed in this field, you should have computer skills, the ability to concentrate for long periods of time on repetitive tasks, good English and communication skills, and mathematical abilities. Legible handwriting is also a necessity.

Certification or Licensing

The International Association of Administrative Professionals offers certification for administrative professionals (including office clerks). Contact the association for more information.

Other Requirements

To find work as an office clerk, you should have an even temperament, strong communication skills, and the ability to work well with others. You should find systematic and detailed work appealing. Other personal qualifications include dependability, trustworthiness, and a neat personal appearance.

EXPLORING

You can gain experience by taking on clerical or bookkeeping responsibilities with a school club or other organization. In addition, some school work-study programs may provide opportunities for part-time, on-the-job training with local businesses. You may also be able to get a part-time or summer job in a business office by contacting businesses directly or enlisting the aid of a guidance counselor. Training in the operation of business machinery (computers, word processors, and so on) may be available through evening courses offered by business schools and community colleges.

EMPLOYERS

Approximately 3.2 million office clerks are employed throughout the United States. Major employers include local government; utility companies; health care companies; finance and insurance agencies; real estate; professional, scientific, and technical services companies; and other large firms. Smaller companies also hire office workers and sometimes offer a greater opportunity to gain experience in a variety of clerical tasks.

STARTING OUT

To secure an entry-level position, you should contact businesses or government agencies directly. Newspaper ads and temporary-work agencies are also good sources for finding jobs in this area. Most companies provide on-the-job training, during which company policies and procedures are explained.

ADVANCEMENT

Office clerks usually begin their employment performing routine tasks such as delivering messages and sorting and filing mail. With experience, they may advance to more complicated assignments and assume a greater responsibility for an entire project. Those who demonstrate the desire and ability may move to other clerical positions, such as secretary or receptionist. Clerks with good leadership skills may become group managers or supervisors. To be promoted to a professional occupation such as accountant, a college degree or other specialized training is usually necessary.

The high turnover rate that exists among office clerks increases promotional opportunities. The number and kind of opportunities, however, usually depend on the place of employment and the ability, education, and experience of the employee.

EARNINGS

Salaries for office clerks vary depending on the size and geographic location of the company and the skills of the worker. According to the U.S. Department of Labor, the median salary for full-time office clerks was $24,460 in 2007. The lowest paid 10 percent earned less than $15,490, while the highest paid group earned more than $38,780. Office clerks earned the following mean salaries by industry in 2007: local government, $28,650; general medical and surgical hospitals, $27,380; colleges, universities, and professional schools, $26,070; and elementary and secondary schools, $26,300.

Full-time workers generally also receive paid vacations, health insurance, sick leave, and other benefits.

WORK ENVIRONMENT

As is the case with most office workers, office clerks work an average 40-hour week. They usually work in comfortable surroundings and are provided with modern equipment. Although clerks have a variety of tasks and responsibilities, the job itself can be fairly routine and repetitive. Clerks often interact with accountants and other office personnel and may work under close supervision.

OUTLOOK

Although employment of clerks is expected to grow only about as fast as the average for all careers through 2016, there will still be many jobs available due to the vastness of this field and a high turnover rate. With the increased use of data processing equipment and other types of automated office machinery, more and more employers are hiring people proficient in a variety of office tasks. According to OfficeTeam, the following industries show the strongest demand for qualified administrative staff: technology, financial services, construction, and manufacturing.

Because they are so versatile, office workers can find employment in virtually any kind of industry, so their overall employment does not depend on the fortunes of any single sector of the economy. In addition to private companies, the federal government should continue to be a good source of jobs. Office clerks with excellent computer skills, proficiency in office machinery, strong communication skills, and the ability to perform many tasks at once will be in strong demand. Temporary and part-time work opportunities should also increase, especially during busy business periods.

FOR MORE INFORMATION

For information on seminars, conferences, and news on the industry, contact

Association of Executive and Administrative Professionals
900 South Washington Street, Suite G-13
Falls Church, VA 22046-4009
Tel: 703-237-8616
Email: headquarters@theaeap.com
http:// www.theaeap.com

For information on certification, contact
International Association of Administrative Professionals
PO Box 20404
Kansas City, MO 64195-0404
Tel: 816-891-6600
Email: service@iaap-hq.org
http://www.iaap-hq.org

For free office career and salary information, visit
OfficeTeam
http://www.officeteam.com

Railroad Clerks

OVERVIEW

Railroad clerks perform the clerical duties involved in transacting business and keeping records for railroad companies. Their jobs may involve many different kinds of clerical work or only one or two specialized duties, depending on the size and type of their railroad company or location.

HISTORY

The modern era of railroading began in the early 1800s when two Englishmen, Richard Trevithick and George Stephenson, perfected their versions of the steam locomotive. In the early days railroads were largely short lines, and a few clerks could keep track of the trains' cargo and destinations. But as railroads expanded, both geographically and in the types of freight they could carry, clerks became essential to keep track of what was being hauled where, when it was needed, and who would pay for it. The railroad industry reached a historic climax on May 10, 1869, with the completion of the first transcontinental railway. The Union Pacific Railroad, building west from Nebraska, and the Central Pacific Railroad, building east from California, met at Promontory Point, Utah, where a golden spike was driven to set the merging rails.

Passenger and freight business on the nation's rail lines peaked in the 1920s and 1930s and then went into decline. Still, rail is an important method of transportation. For example, automobile manufacturers use the railroad more than any other means of transportation to ship completed automobiles. Other commodities, such as coal and farm products, still rely heavily on rail. The North American railroad

QUICK FACTS

School Subjects
Business
Computer science
Mathematics

Personal Skills
Communication/ideas
Following instructions

Work Environment
Primarily indoors
Primarily one location

Minimum Education Level
High school diploma

Salary Range
$15,490 to $32,000 to $51,7010+

Certification or Licensing
None available

Outlook
Decline

DOT
237

GOE
09.07.02, 09.08.01

NOC
1476

O*NET-SOC
N/A

system is now a complex, interconnecting network of some 173,000 miles of lines. While computers have eliminated some clerical jobs, clerks are still needed to keep accurate records, compile statistics, and transact railroad business for the complex systems of freight, express, and passenger rail service.

THE JOB

Volumes of paperwork are necessary to keep accurate records and provide information on the business transactions of railroad companies. Railroad clerks are responsible for completing and maintaining this paperwork. They interact with customers of the railroad and railroad employees at all levels.

Traditionally, railroad clerks have been employed in railroad yards, terminals, freight houses, railroad stations, and company offices. However, as railroad companies have merged, and as computers are increasingly used, railroads have tended to consolidate much of their operation into a centralized location. As a result, most railroad clerks no longer work on-site in the terminals; instead, they work at the railroad's central office. The information they need from the various terminals, yards, and stations is transmitted to them via computer and video camera.

Clerks may perform a variety of duties, depending on the size of the company they work for and the level of seniority they have achieved. Railroad clerks employed on Class I "line-haul" railroads perform such clerical duties as selling tickets, bookkeeping, compiling statistics, collecting bills, investigating complaints and adjusting claims, and tracing lost or misdirected shipments. *Yard clerks* use information from records or other personnel to prepare orders for railroad yard switching crews. They also keep records of cars moving into or out of the yard.

Dispatcher clerks schedule train crews for work, notify them of their assignments, and record the time and distance they work.

Train clerks record the exact time each train arrives at or leaves the station, compare those times with schedules, and inquire about reasons for delays. They also process other data about train movements. (Today, computers do much of this tracking, but clerks are still needed to organize and compile the data for reports.)

Railroad-maintenance clerks keep records about repairs being made to tracks or rights-of-way, including the location and type of repair and the materials and time involved.

A great deal of railroad business and income involves moving freight. *Documentation-billing clerks* prepare the billing documents that list a freight shipper's name, the type and weight of cargo, des-

Did You Know?

- There are 565 freight railroads operating in the United States.
- These railroads have 186,812 employees.
- Freight railroads transport more than 40 percent of freight in the United States.
- Freight rail traffic is expected to increase by 88 percent from 2002 to 2035.

Sources: Association of American Railroads, U.S. Department of Transportation

tination, charges, and so on. They total the charges, check for accuracy, and resolve discrepancies. *Demurrage clerks* compute charges for delays in loading or unloading freight, prepare bills for these charges, and send the bills to the shippers or receivers responsible for the delays. They also communicate with shippers and receivers about the time and place of shipment arrival and the time allowed for unloading freight before they levy any charges.

Revising clerks verify and revise freight and tariff charges on shipment bills. *Interline clerks* examine waybills and ticket sales records to compute the charges payable to the various carriers involved in interline business. *Accounts adjustable clerks* compute corrected freight charges from waybill data. *Voucher clerks* receive claims for lost or damaged goods and prorate the cost of the goods to the various carriers involved in an interline shipment. *Express clerks* receive packages from customers, compute charges, write bills, receive payments, issue receipts, and release packages to the proper recipients.

Secretaries, typists, stenographers, bookkeepers, and *operators of business and computing machines* constitute a second group of railroad clerical workers. All of these employees perform clerical duties that are similar to those performed in other types of business and industry.

Thousands of railroad clerks are employed in higher level jobs that require technical skills and knowledge. Such workers might include *collectors,* who pursue uncollected bills; *accountants,* who are concerned with company financial transactions; and *records and statistical clerks,* responsible for statistical compilations on railroad traffic, employees, and other business details. In addition, these employees are also frequently responsible for compiling periodic reports for the federal government on railroad business, transactions, and operational traffic.

Top Freight Revenue by Commodity, 2007

Coal	21 percent
Miscellaneous mixed shipments	14 percent
Chemicals	12 percent
Farm products	8 percent
Transportation equipment	8 percent
Food	7 percent
Steel and other metal products	4 percent
Lumber and wood	4 percent
Pulp and paper	4 percent
Stone and clay products	3 percent
Nonmetallic minerals	3 percent
All others	11 percent

Source: Association of American Railroads

REQUIREMENTS

High School

A high school education is the minimum educational requirement for most railroad clerk positions. You should take business and communication courses, such as English and speech, in high school. Computer science courses are also important.

Postsecondary Training

Students who have postsecondary training in accounting, office management, or computer applications may be in a better position to get hired as a railroad clerk than students with high school diplomas only. In many instances, companies also require that you successfully pass clerical aptitude tests and be able to type 35–40 words per minute. Finally, because computers are now commonplace in the railroad industry, potential clerks will find that they need a certain degree of computer literacy.

Other Requirements

Patience and attention to detail are important for all clerical workers. Since you may regularly work with the public, a congenial disposition, a pleasant phone voice, and the ability to get along well with others are valuable assets. For example, one major railroad, Norfolk

Southern, outlines the following standards for successful candidates for clerk positions: "be responsible and reliable, able to make quick decisions and prioritize work; be energetic and able to handle inquiries with strong interpersonal skills and a customer focus."

EXPLORING

One way to observe railroad clerks at work is to obtain a part-time or summer job with a railroad company as a messenger or office assistant. If a railroad job is not available, working in any sort of office setting might give you experience with clerical work such as typing, stenography, bookkeeping, and the operation of common office equipment.

EMPLOYERS

Railroad clerks may be employed by passenger lines or freight lines. They may work for one of the major railroads, such as Burlington Northern Santa Fe, Norfolk Southern, CSX, or Union Pacific Railroad, or they may work for one of the 500 smaller short line railroads across the country. Clerks who work for a major railroad generally work in a large centralized office with many other workers. Railroad clerks may work in any part of the country, urban or rural. Clerks who are employed by commuter passenger lines work in large metropolitan areas.

STARTING OUT

Railroad companies frequently fill railroad clerical positions by promoting current office assistants or messengers. Therefore, you are most likely to find entrance into the field via a lower level job. Once accepted for employment with a railroad company, you may be given a temporary appointment as an "extra" and listed for "extra board" work until a regular job appointment becomes available.

Individuals interested in railroad clerical jobs may apply directly to the railroad companies or inquire about job application procedures through the union representing this group of employees. Newspaper advertisements may sometimes list openings for clerical employees.

ADVANCEMENT

Seniority plays a key role in advancement within the railroad industry. Jobs with higher pay, better hours, and more responsibility almost always go to those workers who have put in many years with the company. Most clerks are designated trainees for a period of 14–90 days when they first begin working before they advance to full-fledged clerks.

Railroad clerks who have achieved a high level of seniority and who have proven their abilities are sometimes promoted to assistant chief clerks or to positions of higher administrative status. Clerks who continue their formal education and training in some field of specialization, such as accounting or statistics, may have opportunities for promotions into jobs as auditors or statisticians. Other advancement opportunities may include advancement to traffic agent, buyer, storekeeper, or ticket and station agent.

EARNINGS

Salaries for railroad clerks vary depending on union agreements, training, experience, job responsibilities, and the type of operation in which the employee works. In most cases hourly wages are set by the agreement between the railroad and the union. Clerks represented by the Transportation Communications Union earned an average hourly salary of $24.86 in 2008 (or $51,710 annually).

Salaries for office clerks employed in all industries ranged from less than $15,490 to $38,780 or more in 2008, according to the U.S. Department of Labor. The Department reports the following mean salaries in 2007 for clerks by specialty: production, planning, and expediting clerks, $41,050; cargo and freight agents, $38,760; dispatchers, $35,500; bookkeeping, accounting, and auditing clerks, $32,780; bill and account collectors, $31,630; reservation and transportation ticket agents and travel clerks, $31,080; customer service representatives, $31,040; and shipping, receiving, and traffic clerks, $28,410.

Railroad employees are usually paid time and a half for any time worked over eight hours a day. Most railroad employees are given paid vacation, sick days, and holidays. Retired railroad workers receive pensions and retirement insurance from the U.S. Railroad Retirement Administration, which they pay into while they are working.

WORK ENVIRONMENT

A 40-hour workweek is the typical schedule for railroad clerical employees in nonsupervisory positions. Individuals who have temporary appointments may have an irregular work schedule, depending on the type of railroad setting in which they are employed. Clerks are sometimes expected to be available to work in a three-shift operation. Many clerks work strictly during the day, though. The majority of these workers perform their duties in comfortable, well-lit offices or stations. Large company offices may be more elaborately furnished and equipped than those of smaller stations.

The work of railroad clerks is not considered hazardous or physically strenuous; much of it is done while sitting down. Some types of clerical work can be tedious and unexciting, however, and in some cases, they can result in eyestrain. Some clerks have to interact with the public, either by phone, via email, or in person. These workers are exposed to various personalities, some of which may be quite difficult.

OUTLOOK

Railroad clerks have been hit hard by the overall decline in railroad business; in the last 15 years, the total number of clerks employed has decreased by 50–60 percent. The increasing use of electronic data processing and computers have also played a large part in the employment decline for these workers, as machines and computers have come to do more of the freight bill processing and recording of information on freight movements and yard operations.

Although this decline in employment is expected to continue over the next several years, some job opportunities are expected to become available each year for these workers. According to the Association of American Railroads, railroads still account for more than 40 percent of all freight transportation in the United States—which will continue to create demand for qualified clerks. Job turnover in this occupational group is relatively high as a result of retirements and employees transferring to other fields.

FOR MORE INFORMATION

For general information on the railroad industry, contact
Association of American Railroads
50 F Street, NW
Washington, DC 20001-1564
Tel: 202-639-2100
http://www.aar.org

For information on the career of railroad clerk, contact
Transportation Communications International Union
Three Research Place
Rockville, MD 20850-3279
Tel: 301-948-4910
http://www.tcunion.org

Real Estate Clerks

QUICK FACTS

School Subjects
Business
English
Mathematics

Personal Skills
Communication/ideas
Following instructions

Work Environment
Primarily indoors
Primarily one location

Minimum Education Level
High school diploma

Salary Range
$22,290 to $24,110 to
$28,440+

Certification or Licensing
Voluntary

Outlook
More slowly than the average

DOT
219

GOE
09.07.02

NOC
1411

O*NET-SOC
43-9061.00

OVERVIEW

Real estate clerks perform a variety of clerical tasks that help real estate-related businesses, such as realtors and construction firms, run smoothly.

HISTORY

There has always been a need for clerks in the real estate industry, but technological advances (including the Internet and the use of databases such as the Multiple Listing Service) have increased the need for qualified clerks. Today, clerks play a key role in the real estate industry—helping construction managers, realtors, and other industry professionals do their jobs quickly and efficiently.

THE JOB

Real estate clerks perform a wide variety of tasks that help real estate agents, construction managers, construction inspectors, building managers, and other real estate professionals do their jobs. These tasks include maintaining files; sorting mail; drafting correspondence; keeping records; typing copies of lists of rental or sales properties for submission to real estate databases or for listing in newspaper want ads; answering telephone calls about available properties or a need for services; making photocopies; preparing mailings (including announcements for open houses or rent notices to tenants); operating office equipment such as photocopiers, fax machines, and switchboards; computing, classifying, recording, and verifying financial data; and producing and processing bills and collecting payments from customers.

A real estate clerk records property deeds. *(Bob Daemmrich/The Image Works)*

In small companies, real estate clerks perform most or all of the aforementioned duties. In larger companies, clerks may have more specialized duties. The following paragraphs detail the specialties available for people who work as clerks in the real estate industry.

File clerks review and classify letters, documents, articles, and other information and then file this material so it can be quickly retrieved at a later time. This information may be in electronic or paper format.

Billing clerks keep records and up-to-date accounts of all business transactions. They type and send bills for services or products and update files to reflect payments. They also review incoming invoices to ensure that the requested products have been delivered and that the billing statements are accurate and paid on time.

Bookkeeping clerks keep systematic records and current accounts of financial transactions for real estate management companies and developers. The bookkeeping records of a firm or business are a vital part of its operational procedures because these records reflect the firm's assets and the liabilities, as well as its profits and losses.

REQUIREMENTS

High School

Take courses in English, mathematics, and as many business-related subjects, such as keyboarding and bookkeeping, as possible to prepare for this career.

Postsecondary Training

A high school diploma is usually sufficient to enter this field, but clerks who have received postsecondary training covering office machine operation and bookkeeping will have the best employment prospects. These courses are offered by business schools and community colleges.

Certification or Licensing

Although there is no specific certification available for real estate clerks, the International Association of Administrative Professionals offers certification for general administrative professionals (including office clerks). Contact the association for more information.

Other Requirements

Successful real estate clerks have strong computer skills, are excellent communicators, and are able to concentrate on repetitive tasks for long periods of time. They also have the ability to work well with others and are dependable, trustworthy, and have a neat personal appearance.

EXPLORING

A good way to learn more about the work of clerks is to perform clerical or bookkeeping tasks for a school club or organization. Your school may also have a school-to-work program that can provide you with part-time, on-the-job training with local businesses, such as real estate agencies, newspapers and magazines that focus on the real estate industry, law firms that specialize in real estate, and financial institutions. You might also ask your school counselor to help arrange an information interview with a clerk—especially one who is employed in the real estate industry.

EMPLOYERS

Major employers include real estate agencies, real estate developers, finance and insurance companies, advertising agencies, local government, health care and social assistance organizations, administrative and support services companies, and professional, scientific, and technical services industries.

STARTING OUT

To secure an entry-level position, contact real estate-related companies directly. Newspaper ads and temporary-work agencies are also good sources for finding jobs in this field.

ADVANCEMENT

Real estate clerks typically advance by learning new skills and being tasked with more complicated assignments. Clerks who demonstrate leadership ability may be asked to supervise other clerks, while others may be promoted to different clerical positions, such as secretary or receptionist. Some clerks may earn a college degree or other specialized training in order to advance to professional positions such as accountant, real estate agent, or construction manager.

EARNINGS

Salaries for real estate clerks vary depending on the size and geographic location of the company and the skills of the worker. According to Salary.com, the median salary for full-time real estate clerks was $24,110 in 2008. The lowest paid 10 percent earned less than $22,290, while the highest paid group earned more than $28,440.

Benefits for real estate clerks depend on the employer; however, they usually include such items as health insurance, retirement or 401(k) plans, and paid vacation days.

WORK ENVIRONMENT

Most real estate clerks work an average of 37 to 40 hours per week. Clerks in the real estate industry may work evenings and weekends, as much of the business conducted in this field occurs during nontraditional business hours. Although clerks perform a variety of tasks, the job itself can be fairly routine and repetitive. Clerks often interact with accountants, real estate agents, and other office personnel and may work under close supervision.

OUTLOOK

Although employment of all types of office clerks is expected to grow about as fast as the average for all occupations through 2016, there will be fewer opportunities for real estate clerks due to difficult economic times that have slowed home and business sales throughout the United States. Clerks who pursue jobs in industries that have a more promising employment outlook will have the best opportunities.

Despite this prediction, there will still be jobs available for real estate clerks due to the size of this field and a high turnover rate. Opportunities will be best for clerks who have strong computer skills and knowledge of business software that is commonly used in the real estate industry.

FOR MORE INFORMATION

For information on seminars, conferences, and news on the industry, contact
Association of Executive and Administrative Professionals
900 South Washington Street, Suite G-13
Falls Church, VA 22046-4009
Tel: 703-237-8616
Email: headquarters@theaeap.com
http://www.theaeap.com

For information on certification, contact
International Association of Administrative Professionals
PO Box 20404
Kansas City, MO 64195-0404
Tel: 816-891-6600
Email: service@iaap-hq.org
http://www.iaap-hq.org

For information on the real estate industry, contact
National Association of Realtors
430 North Michigan Avenue

Chicago, IL 60611-4011
Tel: 800-874-6500
http://www.realtor.org

For free office career and salary information and job listings, visit
OfficeTeam
http://www.officeteam.com

Receptionists

QUICK FACTS

School Subjects
Business
Computer science
English

Personal Skills
Communication/ideas
Following instructions

Work Environment
Primarily indoors
Primarily one location

Minimum Education Level
High school diploma

Salary Range
$16,290 to $23,710 to
$34,470+

Certification or Licensing
None available

Outlook
Faster than the average

DOT
237

GOE
09.05.01

NOC
1414

O*NET-SOC
43-4171.00

OVERVIEW

Receptionists—so named because they receive visitors in places of business—have the important job of giving a business's clients and visitors a positive first impression. These front-line workers are the first communication sources in a business, greeting clients and visitors, answering their questions, and directing them to the people they wish to see. Receptionists also answer telephones, take and distribute messages for other employees, and make sure no one enters the office unescorted or unauthorized. Many receptionists perform additional clerical duties. *Switchboard operators* perform similar tasks but primarily handle equipment that receives an organization's telephone calls. There are approximately 1.2 million receptionists employed throughout the United States.

HISTORY

In the 18th and 19th centuries merchants and other business people began to recognize the importance of giving customers the immediate impression that the business was friendly, efficient, and trustworthy. These businesses began to employ hosts and hostesses, workers who would greet customers, make them comfortable, and often serve them refreshments while they waited or did business with the owner. As businesses grew larger and more diverse, these hosts and hostesses (only recently renamed receptionists) took on the additional duties of answering phones, keeping track of workers, and directing visitors to the employee they needed to see. Receptionists took on an expanded role as information workers, answering growing numbers of inquiries from the public.

In the medical field, as services expanded, more receptionists were needed to direct patients to physicians and clinical services and to keep track of appointments and payment information.

Soon receptionists became indispensable to business and service establishments. Today, it is hard to imagine most medium-sized or large businesses functioning without a receptionist.

THE JOB

The receptionist is a specialist in human contact. The most important part of a receptionist's job is dealing with people in a courteous and effective manner. Receptionists greet customers, clients, patients, and salespeople, take their names, and determine the nature of their business and the person they wish to see. The receptionist then pages the requested person, directs the visitor to that person's office or location, or makes an appointment for a later visit. Receptionists often keep records of all visits by writing down the visitor's name, purpose of visit, person visited, and date and time.

Most receptionists answer the telephone at their place of employment; many operate switchboards or paging systems. These workers usually take and distribute messages for other employees and may receive and distribute mail. Receptionists may perform a variety of other clerical duties, including keying in and filing correspondence and other paperwork, proofreading, preparing travel vouchers, and preparing outgoing mail. In some businesses, receptionists are responsible for monitoring the attendance of other employees. In businesses where employees are frequently out of the office on assignments, receptionists may keep track of their whereabouts to ensure they receive important phone calls and messages. Many receptionists use computers and word processors to perform clerical duties.

Receptionists are partially responsible for maintaining office security, especially in large firms. They may require all visitors to sign in and out and carry visitors' passes during their stay. Since visitors may not enter most offices unescorted, receptionists usually accept and sign for packages and other deliveries.

Receptionists are frequently responsible for answering inquiries from the public about a business's nature and operations. To answer these questions efficiently and in a manner that conveys a favorable impression, a receptionist must be as knowledgeable as possible about the business's products, services, policies, and practices and familiar with the names and responsibilities of all other employees. They must be careful, however, not to divulge classified information such as business procedures or employee activities that a competing company might be able to use. This part of a receptionist's job is so important that some businesses call their receptionists *information clerks.*

A large number of receptionists work in physicians' and dentists' offices, hospitals, clinics, and other health care establishments. Workers in medical offices receive patients, take their names, and escort them to examination rooms. They make future appointments for patients and may prepare statements and collect bill payments. In hospitals receptionists obtain patient information, assign patients to rooms, and keep records on the dates they are admitted and discharged.

In other types of industries the duties of these workers vary. Receptionists in hair salons arrange appointments for clients and may escort them to stylists' stations. Workers in bus or train companies answer inquiries about departures, arrivals, and routes. In-file operators collect and distribute credit information to clients for credit purposes. Registrars, park aides, and tourist-information assistants may be employed as receptionists at public or private facilities. Their duties may include keeping a record of the visitors entering and leaving the facility, as well as providing information on services that the facility provides. Information clerks, automobile club information clerks, and referral-and-information aides provide answers to questions by telephone or in person from both clients and potential clients and keep a record of all inquiries.

Switchboard operators may perform specialized work, such as operating switchboards at police district offices. Or, they may handle airport communication systems, which includes public-address paging systems and courtesy telephones, or serve as answering-service operators, who record and deliver messages for clients who cannot be reached by telephone.

REQUIREMENTS

High School
You can prepare for a receptionist position by taking courses in business, business math, English, and public speaking. You should also take computer science courses.

Postsecondary Training
Most employers require receptionists to have a high school diploma. Some businesses prefer to hire workers who have completed post-high school courses at a junior college or business school. Courses in basic bookkeeping and principles of accounting will be helpful. This type of training may lead to a higher paying receptionist job and

Successful receptionists have pleasant personalities and excellent communication skills. *(Scott Stulberg/Corbis)*

a better chance for advancement. Many employers require typing, switchboard, computer, and other clerical skills, but they may provide some on-the-job training, as the work is typically entry level.

Other Requirements
To be a good receptionist, you must be well groomed, have a pleasant voice, and be able to express yourself clearly. Because you may sometimes deal with demanding people, a smooth, patient disposition

and good judgment are important. All receptionists need to be courteous and tactful. A good memory for faces and names also proves very valuable. Most important are good listening and communication skills and an understanding of human nature.

EXPLORING

A good way to obtain experience as a receptionist is through a high school work-study program. Students participating in such programs spend part of their school day in classes and the rest working for local businesses. This arrangement will help you gain valuable practical experience before you look for your first job. High school guidance counselors can provide information about work-study opportunities.

EMPLOYERS

According to the U.S. Department of Labor, approximately 1.2 million people are employed as receptionists. Factories, wholesale and retail stores, and service providers employ a large percentage of these workers. Approximately 33 percent of the receptionists in the United States work in health care settings, including offices, hospitals, nursing homes, urgent care centers, and clinics. More than 30 percent work part time.

STARTING OUT

While you are in high school, you may be able to learn of openings with local businesses through your school guidance counselors or newspaper want ads. Local state employment offices frequently have information about receptionist work. You should also contact area businesses for whom you would like to work; many available positions are not advertised in the paper because they are filled so quickly. Temporary-work agencies are a valuable resource for finding jobs.

ADVANCEMENT

Advancement opportunities are limited for receptionists, especially in small offices. The more clerical skills and education workers have, the greater their chances for promotion to such better paying jobs as secretary, administrative assistant, or bookkeeper. College or business school training can help receptionists advance to higher level positions. Many companies provide training for their receptionists and other employees, helping workers gain skills for job advancement.

EARNINGS

Earnings for receptionists vary widely with the education and experience of the worker and type, size, and geographic location of the business. The U.S. Department of Labor reported that in 2007 the median salary for receptionists was $23,710. The lowest paid 10 percent of these workers made less than $16,290 annually, while the highest paid 10 percent earned more than $34,470 per year. Receptionists are usually eligible for paid holidays and vacations, sick leave, medical and life insurance coverage, and a retirement plan of some kind.

WORK ENVIRONMENT

Receptionists usually work near or at the main entrance to the business. Therefore, these areas are usually pleasant and clean and are carefully furnished and decorated to create a favorable, businesslike impression. Work areas are almost always air-conditioned, well lit, and relatively quiet, although a receptionist's phone rings frequently. Receptionists work behind a desk or counter and spend most of their workday sitting, although some standing and walking is required when filing or escorting visitors to their destinations. The job may be stressful at times, especially when a worker must be polite to rude callers.

Most receptionists work Monday through Friday, 35–40 hours a week. Some may work weekend and evening hours, especially those in medical offices. Switchboard operators may have to work any shift of the day if their employers require 24-hour phone service, such as hotels and hospitals. These workers usually work holidays and weekend hours.

OUTLOOK

Employment for receptionists is expected to grow faster than the average for all careers through 2016, according to the *Occupational Outlook Handbook*. Many openings will occur due to the occupation's high turnover rate. Opportunities will be best for those with work experience and a variety of clerical skills. Growth in jobs for receptionists is expected to be greater than for other clerical positions because automation will have little effect on the receptionist's largely interpersonal duties and because of an anticipated growth in the number of businesses providing services. In addition, more and more businesses know how a receptionist can convey a positive public image. Opportunities should be especially good in physician's offices, law firms, temporary help agencies, and management and technical consulting firms.

FOR MORE INFORMATION

For information on careers, contact
International Association of Administrative Professionals
PO Box 20404
Kansas City, MO 64195-0404
Tel: 816-891-6600
Email: service@iaap-hq.org
http://www.iaap-hq.org

For free office career and salary information, visit
OfficeTeam
http://www.officeteam.com

Secretaries

OVERVIEW

Secretaries, or *administrative assistants*, perform a wide range of jobs that vary greatly from business to business. However, most secretaries key in documents, manage records and information, answer telephones, send and respond to emails and faxes, handle correspondence, schedule appointments, make travel arrangements, and sort mail. The amount of time secretaries spend on these duties depends on the size and type of the office as well as on their own job training. There are approximately 4.2 million secretaries employed in the United States.

HISTORY

People have always needed to communicate with one another for societies to function efficiently. Today, as in the past, secretaries play an important role in keeping lines of communication open. Before there were telephones, messages were transmitted by hand, often from the secretary of one party to the secretary of the receiving party. Their trustworthiness was valued because the lives of many people often hung in the balance of certain communications.

Secretaries in the ancient world developed methods of taking abbreviated notes so that they could capture as much as possible of their employers' words. The modern precursors of the shorthand methods we know today developed in 16th-century England. In the 19th century Isaac Pitman and John Robert Gregg developed the shorthand systems that are still used in offices and courtrooms in the United States.

QUICK FACTS

School Subjects
Business
Computer science
English

Personal Skills
Communication/ideas
Following instructions

Work Environment
Primarily indoors
Primarily one location

Minimum Education Level
High school diploma

Salary Range
$17,920 to $28,220 to $60,800+

Certification or Licensing
Voluntary

Outlook
About as fast as the average

DOT
201

GOE
09.02.02

NOC
1241

O*NET-SOC
43-6012.00, 43-6013.00, 43-6014.00

The equipment secretaries use in their work has changed drastically in recent years. Almost every office, from the smallest to the largest, is automated in some way. Familiarity with machines including switchboards, photocopiers, fax machines, videoconferencing and telephone systems, scanners, and personal computers has become an integral part of the secretary's day-to-day work.

THE JOB

Secretaries perform a variety of administrative and clerical duties. The goal of all their activities is to assist their employers in the execution of their work and to help their companies conduct business in an efficient and professional manner.

Secretaries' work includes processing and transmitting information to the office staff and to other organizations. They operate office machines and arrange for their repair or servicing. These machines include computers, typewriters, dictating machines, photocopiers, switchboards, and fax machines. These secretaries also order office supplies and perform regular duties such as answering phones, sorting mail, managing files, taking dictation, and composing and keying in letters.

Some offices have word processing centers that handle all of the firm's typing. In such a situation, *administrative secretaries* take care of all secretarial duties except for typing and dictation. This arrangement leaves them free to respond to correspondence, prepare reports, do research and present the results to their employers, and otherwise assist the professional staff. Often these secretaries work in groups of three or four so that they can help each other if one secretary has a workload that is heavier than normal.

In many offices secretaries make appointments for company executives and keep track of the office schedule. They make travel arrangements for the professional staff or for clients, and occasionally are asked to travel with staff members on business trips. Other secretaries might manage the office while their supervisors are away on vacation or business trips.

Secretaries take minutes at meetings, write up reports, and compose and type letters. They often will find their responsibilities growing as they learn the business. Some are responsible for finding speakers for conferences, planning receptions, and arranging public relations programs. Some write copy for brochures or articles before making the arrangements to have them printed, or they might use desktop publishing software to create the documents themselves. They greet clients and guide them to the proper offices, and they often supervise

A school secretary reviews files before a meeting. *(David Bacon/ The Image Works)*

and train other staff members and newer secretaries, especially on how to use computer software programs.

Some secretaries perform very specialized work. *Legal secretaries* prepare legal papers including wills, mortgages, contracts, deeds, motions, complaints, and summonses. They work under the direct supervision of an attorney or paralegal. They assist with legal research by reviewing legal journals and organizing briefs for their employers. They must learn an entire specialized vocabulary that is used in legal papers and documents. For more information on this career, see the article "Legal Secretaries."

Medical secretaries take medical histories of patients, make appointments, prepare and send bills to patients (as well as track and collect them), process insurance billing, maintain medical files, and pursue correspondence with patients, hospitals, and associations. They assist physicians or medical scientists with articles, reports, speeches, and conference proceedings. Some medical secretaries are responsible for ordering medical supplies. They, too, need to learn an entire specialized vocabulary of medical terms and be familiar with laboratory or hospital procedures. For more information on this career, see the article "Medical Secretaries."

Technical secretaries work for engineers and scientists. They prepare reports and papers that often include graphics and mathematical equations that are difficult to format on paper. The secretaries maintain a technical library and help with scientific papers by gathering and editing materials.

Executive secretaries provide support for top executives. They perform fewer clerical duties and more information management-related duties. Their duties include managing clerical staff; assessing memos, reports, and other documents in order to determine their importance for distribution; preparing meeting agendas; and conducting research and preparing reports.

Social secretaries, often called *personal secretaries*, arrange all of the social activities of their employers. They handle private as well as business social affairs, and they may plan parties, send out invitations, or write speeches for their employers. Social secretaries often work for celebrities or high-level executives who have busy social calendars to maintain.

Many associations, clubs, and nonprofit organizations have *membership secretaries* who compile and send out newsletters or promotional materials while maintaining membership lists, dues records, and directories. Depending on the type of club, the secretary may be the one who gives out information to prospective members and who keeps current members and related organizations informed of upcoming events.

Education secretaries work in elementary or secondary schools or on college campuses. They take care of all clerical duties at the school. Their responsibilities may include preparing bulletins and reports for teachers, parents, or students, keeping track of budgets for school supplies or student activities, and maintaining the school's calendar of events. Depending on the position, they may work for school administrators, principals, or groups of teachers or professors. Other education secretaries work in administration offices, state education departments, or service departments.

REQUIREMENTS

High School

You will need at least a high school diploma to enter this field. To prepare for a career as a secretary, take high school courses including business, English, and speech. Keyboarding and computer science courses will also be helpful.

Postsecondary Training

To succeed as a secretary, you will need good office skills that include rapid and accurate keyboarding skills and good spelling and grammar. You should enjoy handling details. Some positions require typ-

Responsibilities and Career Prospects Improving for Administrative Workers

Seventy-three percent of managers surveyed in 2008 by Office-Team reported that the responsibilities of their support workers had increased "significantly" or "somewhat" in the past five years. "Efficiencies created by technological advancements have allowed administrative assistants to take on a wider range of tasks, including managing budgets, negotiating vendor contracts, overseeing projects, and maintaining Web sites," said Dave Willmer, executive director of OfficeTeam.

The added responsibilities have translated into improved career opportunities for many administrative workers, according to the survey. Fifty-seven percent of respondents believed that administrative workers had more of a career-growth track than they did five years ago.

ing a minimum number of words per minute, as well as shorthand ability. Knowledge of word processing, spreadsheets, and database management is important, and many employers require it. You can learn some of these skills in business education courses taught at vocational and business schools.

Certification or Licensing

Qualifying for the designation certified professional secretary rating is increasingly recognized in business and industry as a consideration for promotion as a senior-level secretary. The International Association of Administrative Professionals administers the examinations required for this certification. Secretaries with limited experience can become an accredited legal secretary by obtaining certification from NALS...the association for legal professionals. Those with at least three years of experience in the legal field can be certified as a professional legal secretary from this same organization. Legal Secretaries International offers the certified legal secretary specialist designation in the following categories: business law, civil litigation, criminal law, intellectual property, probate, and real estate.

Other Requirements

Personal qualities are important in this field of work. As a secretary, you will often be the first employee of a company that clients meet, and therefore you must be friendly, poised, and professionally dressed. Because you must work closely with others, you should be personable and tactful. Discretion, good judgment, organizational ability, and initiative are also important. These traits will not only get you hired but will also help you advance in your career.

Some employers encourage their secretaries to take advanced courses and to be trained to use any new piece of equipment in the office. Requirements vary widely from company to company.

EXPLORING

High school guidance counselors can give you interest and aptitude tests to help you assess your suitability for a career as a secretary. Local business schools often welcome visitors and sometimes offer courses that can be taken in conjunction with a high school business course. Work-study programs will also provide you with an opportunity to work in a business setting to get a sense of the work performed by secretaries.

Part-time or summer jobs as receptionists, file clerks, and office clerks are often available in various offices. These jobs are the best indicators of future satisfaction in the secretarial field. You may find a part-time job if you are computer literate. Cooperative education programs arranged through schools and "temping" through an agency also are valuable ways to acquire experience. In general, any job that teaches basic office skills is helpful.

EMPLOYERS

There are 4.2 million secretaries employed throughout the United States, making this profession one of the largest in the country. Of this total, 275,000 specialize as legal secretaries and 408,000 work as medical secretaries. Secretaries are employed in almost every type of industry. Approximately 90 percent of secretaries work in service industries, including the legal, education, health, financial services, real estate, and business industries, as well as in retail and wholesale trade. Others work in construction and manufacturing. A large number of secretaries are employed by federal, state, and local government agencies.

STARTING OUT

Most people looking for work as secretaries find jobs through the newspaper ads or by applying directly to local businesses. Both private employment offices and state employment services place secretaries, and business schools help their graduates find suitable jobs. Temporary-help agencies are an excellent way to find secretarial jobs, many of which may turn into permanent ones.

ADVANCEMENT

Secretaries often begin by assisting executive secretaries and work their way up by learning the way their business operates. Initial promotions from a secretarial position are usually to jobs such as secretarial supervisor, office manager, or administrative assistant. Depending on other personal qualifications, college courses in business, accounting, or marketing can help the ambitious secretary enter middle and upper management. Training in computer skills can also lead to advancement. Secretaries who become proficient in word processing, for instance, can get jobs as instructors or as sales representatives for software manufacturers.

Many legal secretaries, with additional training and schooling, become paralegals. Secretaries in the medical field can advance into the fields of radiological and surgical records or medical transcription.

EARNINGS

Salaries for secretaries vary widely by region, type of business, and the skill, experience, and level of responsibility of the secretary. Secretaries (except legal, medical, and executive) earned an average of $28,220 annually in 2007, according to the U.S. Department of Labor. Salaries for these workers ranged from a low of $17,920 to a high of more than $42,350. Secretaries employed by the federal government earned a starting salary of $42,950 a year in 2007; those employed in local government earned $32,570.

Medical secretaries earned salaries that ranged from less than $20,260 to $41,860 or more per year in 2007, according to the U.S. Department of Labor. Legal secretaries made an average of $38,810 in 2007. Salaries for legal secretaries ranged from $24,380 to more than $60,800 annually. An attorney's rank in the firm will also affect the earnings of a legal secretary; secretaries who work for a partner will earn higher salaries than those who work for an associate.

Secretaries, especially those working in the legal profession, earn considerably more if certified.

Most secretaries receive paid holidays and two weeks vacation after a year of work, as well as sick leave. Many offices provide benefits including health and life insurance, pension plans, overtime pay, and tuition reimbursement.

WORK ENVIRONMENT

Most secretaries work in pleasant offices with modern equipment. Office conditions vary widely, however. While some secretaries have their own offices and work for one or two executives, others share crowded workspace with other workers.

Most office workers work 35 to 40 hours a week. Very few secretaries work on the weekends on a regular basis, although some may be asked to work overtime if a particular project demands it.

The work is not physically strenuous or hazardous, although deadline pressure is a factor and sitting for long periods of time can be uncomfortable. Many hours spent in front of a computer can lead to eyestrain or repetitive-motion problems for secretaries. Most secretaries are not required to travel. Part-time and flexible schedules are easily adaptable to secretarial work.

OUTLOOK

The U.S. Department of Labor predicts that employment for secretaries who specialize in the medical field or who work as executive secretaries will grow faster than the average for all careers through 2016. Employment for legal secretaries and general secretaries is expected to grow about as fast as the average through 2016.

Computers, fax machines, email, copy machines, and scanners are some technological advancements that have greatly improved the work productivity of secretaries. Company downsizing and restructuring, in some cases, have redistributed traditional secretarial duties to other employees. There has been a growing trend in assigning one secretary to assist two or more managers, adding to this field's decline. Though more professionals are using personal computers for their correspondence, some administrative duties will still need to be handled by secretaries. The personal aspects of the job and responsibilities such as making travel arrangements, scheduling conferences, and transmitting staff instructions have not changed.

Many employers currently complain of a shortage of capable secretaries. Those with skills and experience will have the best chances for employment. Specialized secretaries should attain certification in their field to stay competitive.

Industries such as professional, scientific, and technical services; health care and social services; and administrative and support services will create the most new job opportunities. As common with large occupations, the need to replace retiring workers will generate many openings.

FOR MORE INFORMATION

For information on the certified professional secretary designation, contact
International Association of Administrative Professionals
PO Box 20404
Kansas City, MO 64195-0404
Tel: 816-891-6600
Email: service@iaap-hq.org
http://www.iaap-hq.org

For information about certification, contact
Legal Secretaries International
2302 Fannin Street, Suite 500
Houston, TX 77002-9136
http://www.legalsecretaries.org

The Mayo Clinic is a major employer of medical secretaries. Visit its Web site for more information.
Mayo Clinic
http://www.mayo.edu

For information on certification, job openings, a variety of careers in law, and more, contact
NALS...the association for legal professionals
8159 East 41st Street
Tulsa, OK 74145-3313
Tel: 918-582-5188
Email: info@nals.org
http://www.nals.org

For information regarding union representation, contact
Office and Professional Employees International Union
265 West 14th Street, 6th Floor
New York, NY 10011-7103
Tel: 800-346-7348
http://www.opeiu.org

For employment information, contact
OfficeTeam
http://www.officeteam.com

Statistical Clerks

QUICK FACTS

School Subjects
Business
Computer science
Mathematics

Personal Skills
Following instructions
Technical/scientific

Work Environment
Primarily indoors
Primarily one location

Minimum Education Level
High school diploma

Salary Range
$15,000 to $32,540 to
$50,620+

Certification or Licensing
None available

Outlook
Decline

DOT
216

GOE
02.06.02

NOC
1454

O*NET-SOC
43-9111.00

OVERVIEW

Statistical clerks perform routine tasks associated with data collection, data file management, data entry, and data processing. They work in a number of different industries, including advertising, insurance, manufacturing, and health care, to compile and manage information. There are approximately 19,200 statistical clerks employed in the United States.

HISTORY

According to the earliest records, the study of mathematics was developed to meet the practical business needs of farmers and merchants between 3000 and 2000 B.C. in Egypt and Mesopotamia. One branch of applied mathematics, statistics, deals with the collection and classification of various data by certain numerical characteristics. This information is then used to make inferences and predictions in related situations. A relatively young discipline, statistics emerged in 1892 with the publication of *The Grammar of Science*. Its author, Karl Pearson, a mathematics professor at the University of London, is generally regarded as the father of statistics.

Statistics is widely used in many types of businesses today. Insurance companies use statistics to determine the probability of accidents and deaths in order to set reasonable premium rates for their policyholders. Statistics is used to determine the audience ratings of television shows, the popularity of Web sites, and approval ratings of politicians. It can be used in disease prevention and economic projections. As business decisions increasingly depend on demographics and other information that can be tabulated, statistical clerks will continue to play a role in the compilation of relevant data.

THE JOB

Statistical clerks are involved in record keeping and data retrieval. They compile numerical information (questionnaire results and production records, for example) and tabulate it using statistical formulas so that it can be used for further study. They also perform data entry and data processing on computers and are responsible for quality control of the collected data. With the advanced statistical software programs now available, almost all statistical clerks use computers in their work. They also perform clerical functions, such as filing and file management.

Statistical clerks work in a number of fields in a variety of jobs. *Compilers* analyze raw data gathered from surveys, census data, and other reports and organize them into specified categories or groupings. These statistics are compiled into survey findings or census reports. Compilers may prepare graphs or charts to illustrate their findings.

Advertising statistical clerks tabulate statistical records for companies on the cost, volume, and effectiveness of the companies' advertising. They often compare the amount of their customers' merchandise that is sold before an advertising campaign to the amount sold after the campaign to determine whether the campaign influenced consumer behavior.

Medical record clerks and technicians tabulate statistics to be used by medical researchers. They also compile, verify, and file the medical records of hospital or clinic patients and make sure that these records are complete and up to date. Medical record technicians may also assist in compiling the necessary information used in completing hospital insurance billing forms.

Chart calculators work for power companies. They record the net amount of electric power used by the company's customers to check that the correct rates are being charged. They enter power usage information on record forms so that customers are billed at the appropriate rates. *Chart clerks* compile records measuring the quantity of natural or manufactured gas produced, transported, and sold to calculate the volume of gas and petroleum that flows through specific pipelines.

Chart changers record data from instruments that measure industrial processes. They are also responsible for maintaining these recording instruments, such as pyrometers and flowmeters.

Actuarial clerks compile data on insurance policies, rates, and claims so that insurance commissioners and companies know how to set their rates.

REQUIREMENTS

High School
A high school diploma is usually sufficient for beginning statistical clerks. High school students should take courses in English, mathematics, and science, as well as business-related courses such as keyboarding and bookkeeping. Computer use is a vital part of this career, so it is important to take as many basic computer courses as you can.

Postsecondary Training
Many community colleges and vocational schools offer business education courses that provide additional training for statistical clerks in the areas of data processing and office procedures. Taking additional computer classes to learn word processing, database, and spreadsheet programs will also be very helpful. As in most career fields, clerks who have obtained further education and have proven their capabilities typically have more advancement opportunities.

Other Requirements
Prospective clerks need to have some mechanical aptitude in order to be able to operate computers and other office equipment. The ability to concentrate for long periods of time on sometimes repetitive tasks is also important. You should find systematic and orderly work appealing and enjoy working on detailed tasks. In addition, you should work well both independently and with others.

EXPLORING

If you are interested in a career as a statistical clerk, you might gain related experience by taking on clerical or bookkeeping responsibilities with a school club or other organization. In addition, some work-study programs may offer partnerships with businesses for part-time, on-the-job training. You can also contact businesses directly to find a part-time or summer job in an office.

To learn how to operate business machinery and computer software programs, you might consider taking an evening course offered by a local business school or community college. There you might establish business contacts in the classroom, either through other students or through your teacher. To gain insight into the responsibilities of a statistical clerk, talk to someone already working in the field about the job and how he or she got started.

EMPLOYERS

Approximately 19,200 statistical clerks are employed in the United States. In general, statistical clerks are employed by the same sorts of organizations that hire statisticians. The federal government hires statisticians in such areas as the Departments of Commerce, Health and Human Services, and Agriculture. Various sectors of private industry also hire both statisticians and statistical clerks. Private-industry employers include insurance companies, utility research and testing services, management and public relations firms, computer and data processing firms, manufacturing companies, and financial services firms. Other statistical clerks may work for researchers in colleges or universities.

STARTING OUT

When looking for an entry-level statistical clerk's job, you might first scan the help wanted sections of area newspapers. Another avenue for job seekers is to contact the personnel or human resources offices of businesses or government agencies directly.

Most companies provide entry-level statistical clerks with on-the-job training, during which company policy and procedures are explained. Beginning clerks work with experienced personnel during this period.

ADVANCEMENT

In many instances statistical clerks begin their employment as general office clerks; with experience and further training, they become statistical clerks. Also with experience, they may receive more complicated assignments and assume a greater responsibility for the total statistical work to be completed. Those with leadership skills may become group managers or supervisors. In order to become an accountant or bookkeeper, it is usually necessary to get a degree or have other specialized training.

The high turnover rate in this profession increases opportunities for promotion. The number and kinds of opportunities, however, may depend on the place of employment and the ability, training, and experience of the employee.

EARNINGS

Although salaries vary depending on skill, experience, level of responsibility, and geographic location, a newly hired, inexperienced statistical clerk might expect to earn between $15,000 and $20,000 annually. Statistical clerks earned a median salary of $32,540 in 2007, according to the U.S. Department of Labor. The highest paid 10 percent earned $50,620 or more in 2007. Fringe benefits for full-time workers include paid vacations, health insurance, and other benefits.

WORK ENVIRONMENT

Statistical clerks work an average of 40 hours per week, usually in a well-ventilated and well-lighted office. Although statistical clerks perform a variety of tasks, the job itself can be fairly routine and repetitive. Statistical clerks who work at computer monitors for long periods of time may experience some eye and neck strain. Clerks often interact with accountants and other office personnel and may work under close supervision.

OUTLOOK

Employment for statistical clerks is expected to decline through 2016, according to the U.S. Department of Labor. This is a result of new data processing equipment that can do many of the record keeping and data retrieval functions previously performed by statistical clerks. Despite this prediction, however, job openings in this career will be available due to people retiring or otherwise leaving the field. Opportunities should be best for those with training in computers and other types of automated office machinery.

FOR MORE INFORMATION

For information on careers in statistics and schools that offer degrees in statistics, contact
American Statistical Association
732 North Washington Street
Alexandria, VA 22314-1943
Tel: 888-231-3473
Email: asainfo@amstat.org
http://www.amstat.org

For information on schools and career opportunities in statistics in Canada, contact

Statistical Society of Canada
577 King Edward Avenue
Ottawa, ON K1N 6N5 Canada
Tel: 613-562-5320
Email: info@ssc.ca
http://www.ssc.ca

Stock Clerks

QUICK FACTS

School Subjects
English
Mathematics

Personal Skills
Following instructions

Work Environment
Primarily indoors
Primarily one location

Minimum Education Level
High school diploma

Salary Range
$15,080 to $20,490 to
$34,190+

Certification or Licensing
None available

Outlook
Decline

DOT
222

GOE
09.08.01

NOC
1474

O*NET-SOC
43-5081.00, 43-5081.01,
43-5081.02, 43-5081.03,
43-5081.04

OVERVIEW

Stock clerks receive, unpack, store, distribute, and record the inventory for materials or products used by a company, plant, or store. Approximately 1.7 million stock clerks are employed in the United States.

HISTORY

Almost every type of business establishment imaginable—shoe store, restaurant, hotel, auto repair shop, hospital, supermarket, or steel mill—buys materials or products from outside distributors and uses these materials in its operations. A large part of the company's money is tied up in these inventory stocks, but without them operations would come to a standstill. Stores would run out of merchandise to sell, mechanics would be unable to repair cars until new parts were shipped in, and factories would be unable to operate once their basic supply of raw materials ran out.

To avoid these problems, businesses have developed their own inventory-control systems to store enough goods and raw materials for uninterrupted operations, move these materials to the places they are needed, and know when it is time to order more. These systems are the responsibility of stock clerks.

THE JOB

Stock clerks work in just about every type of industry, and no matter what kind of storage or stock room they staff—food, clothing, merchandise, medicine, or raw materials—the work of stock clerks is essentially the same. They receive, sort, put away, distribute, and keep track of the items a business sells or uses. Their titles sometimes vary based on their responsibilities.

When goods are received in a stockroom, stock clerks unpack the shipment and check the contents against documents such as the invoice, purchase order, and bill of lading, which lists the contents of the shipment. The shipment is inspected, and any damaged goods are set aside. Stock clerks may reject or send back damaged items or call vendors to complain about the condition of the shipment. In large companies a *shipping and receiving clerk* may do this work.

Once the goods are received, stock clerks organize them and sometimes mark them with identifying codes or prices so they can be placed in stock according to the existing inventory system. In this way the materials or goods can be found readily when needed, and inventory control is much easier. In many firms stock clerks use hand-held scanners and computers to keep inventory records up to date.

In retail stores and supermarkets, stock clerks may bring merchandise to the sales floor and stock shelves and racks. In stockrooms and warehouses they store materials in bins, on the floor, or on shelves. In other settings, such as restaurants, hotels, and factories, stock clerks deliver goods when they are needed. They may do this on a regular schedule or at the request of other employees or supervisors. Although many stock clerks use mechanical equipment, such as forklifts, to move heavy items, some perform strenuous and laborious work. In general, the work of a stock clerk involves much standing, bending, walking, stretching, lifting, and carrying.

When items are removed from the inventory, stock clerks adjust records to reflect the products' use. These records are kept as current as possible, and inventories are periodically checked against these records. Every item is counted, and the totals are compared with the records on hand or the records from the sales, shipping, production, or purchasing departments. This helps identify how fast items are being used, when items must be ordered from outside suppliers, or even whether items are disappearing from the stockroom. Many retail establishments use computerized cash registers that maintain an inventory count automatically as they record the sale of each item.

The duties of stock clerks vary depending on their place of employment. Stock clerks working in small firms perform many different tasks, including shipping and receiving, inventory control, and purchasing. In large firms, responsibilities may be more narrowly defined. More specific job categories include *inventory clerks, stock control clerks, material clerks, order fillers, stock-control clerks, merchandise distributors,* and shipping and receiving clerks.

Employment/Earnings for Stock Clerks by Industry, 2007

Employer	# Employed	Annual Mean Earnings
Grocery stores	418,580	$21,240
Department stores	314,390	$19,750
Other general merchandise stores	175,060	$20,640
Warehousing and storage	58,800	$29,600
Clothing stores	57,410	$19,390

Source: U.S. Department of Labor

At a construction site or factory that uses a variety of raw and finished materials, there are many different types of specialized work for stock clerks. *Tool crib attendants* issue, receive, and store the various hand tools, machine tools, dies, and other equipment used in an industrial establishment. They make sure the tools come back in reasonably good shape and keep track of those that need replacing. *Parts order and stock clerks* purchase, store, and distribute the spare parts needed for motor vehicles and other industrial equipment. *Metal control coordinators* oversee the movement of metal stock and supplies used in producing nonferrous metal sheets, bars, tubing, and alloys. In mining and other industries that regularly use explosives, *magazine keepers* store explosive materials and components safely and distribute them to authorized personnel. In the military, *space and storage clerks* keep track of the weights and amounts of ammunition and explosive components stored in the magazines of an arsenal and check their storage condition.

Many types of stock clerks can be found in other industries. *Parts clerks* handle and distribute spare and replacement parts in repair and maintenance shops. In eyeglass centers, *prescription clerks* select the lens blanks and frames for making eyeglasses and keep inventory stocked at a specified level. In motion picture companies, *property custodians* receive, store, and distribute the props needed for shooting. In hotels and hospitals, *linen room attendants* issue and keep track of inventories of bed linen, tablecloths, and uniforms, while *kitchen clerks* verify the quantity and quality of food products being taken from the storeroom to the kitchen.

Aboard ships, the clerk in charge of receiving and issuing supplies and keeping track of inventory is known as the *storekeeper*.

REQUIREMENTS

High School

Although there are no specific educational requirements for beginning stock clerks, employers prefer to hire high school graduates. Reading and writing skills and a basic knowledge of mathematics are necessary; typing and filing skills are also useful. In the future, as more companies install computerized inventory systems, knowledge of computer operations will be important.

Other Requirements

Good health and good eyesight is important in this field. A willingness to take orders from supervisors and others is necessary for this work, as is the ability to follow directions. Organizational skills and neatness are also important. Depending on where you work, you may be required to join a union. This is especially true of stock clerks who are employed in industrial fields and who work in large cities with a high percentage of union-affiliated companies.

When a stock clerk handles certain types of materials, extra training or certification may be required. Generally those who handle jewelry, liquor, or drugs must be bonded.

A stock clerk in a warehouse checks an incoming shipment. *(Jim West/ The Image Works)*

EXPLORING

The best way to learn about the responsibilities of a stock clerk is to get a part-time or summer job as a sales clerk, stockroom helper, stockroom clerk, or, in some factories, stock chaser. These jobs are relatively easy to get and can help you learn about stock work, as well as about the duties of workers in related positions. This sort of part-time work can also lead to a full-time job.

EMPLOYERS

Approximately 1.7 million people work as stock clerks. Almost 78 percent of stock clerks work in retail and wholesale firms, and the remainder work in hospitals, factories, government agencies, schools, and other organizations. Nearly all sales floor stock clerks are employed in retail establishments, with about two-thirds working in supermarkets.

STARTING OUT

Job openings for stock clerks often are listed in newspaper classified ads. Job seekers should contact the personnel office of the firm looking for stock clerks and fill out an application for employment. School counselors, parents, relatives, and friends also can be good sources for job leads and may be able to give personal references if an employer requires them.

Stock clerks usually receive on-the-job training. New workers start with simple tasks, such as counting and marking stock. The basic responsibilities of the job are usually learned within the first few weeks. As they progress, stock clerks learn to keep records of incoming and outgoing materials, take inventories, and place orders. As wholesale and warehousing establishments convert to automated inventory systems, stock clerks need to be trained to use the new equipment. Stock clerks who bring merchandise to the sales floor and stock shelves and sales racks need little training.

ADVANCEMENT

Stock clerks with ability and determination have a good chance of being promoted to jobs with greater responsibility. In small firms, stock clerks may advance to sales positions or become assistant buyers or purchasing agents. In large firms, stock clerks can advance to more responsible stock-handling jobs, such as invoice clerk, stock control clerk, and procurement clerk.

Furthering one's education can lead to more opportunities for advancement. By studying at a technical or business school or taking home-study courses, stock clerks can prove to their employer that they have the intelligence and ambition to take on more important tasks. More advanced positions, such as warehouse manager and purchasing agent, are usually given to experienced people who have post-high school education.

EARNINGS

Beginning stock clerks usually earn the minimum wage or slightly more. The U.S. Department of Labor reports that stock clerks earned a median annual salary of $20,490 in 2007. Experienced stock clerks can earn anywhere from $15,080 to more than $34,190, with time-and-a-half pay for overtime. Average earnings vary depending on the type of industry and geographic location. Stock clerks working in the retail trade generally earn wages in the middle range. In transportation, utilities, and wholesale businesses, earnings usually are higher; in finance, insurance, real estate, and other types of office services, earnings generally are lower.

Those working for large companies or national chains may receive excellent benefits. After one year of employment, some stock clerks are offered one to two weeks of paid vacation each year, as well as health and medical insurance and a retirement plan.

WORK ENVIRONMENT

Stock clerks usually work in relatively clean, comfortable areas. Working conditions vary considerably, however, depending on the industry and type of merchandise being handled. For example, stock clerks who handle refrigerated goods must spend some time in cold storage rooms, while those who handle construction materials, such as bricks and lumber, occasionally work outside in harsh weather. Most stock clerk jobs involve much standing, bending, walking, stretching, lifting, and carrying. Some workers may be required to operate machinery to lift and move stock.

Because stock clerks are employed in so many different types of industries, the amount of hours worked every week depends on the type of employer. Stock clerks in retail stores usually work a five-day, 40-hour week, while those in industry work 44 hours, or five and one-half days, a week. Many others are able to find part-time work. Overtime is common, especially when large shipments arrive or during peak times such as holiday seasons.

OUTLOOK

Although the volume of inventory transactions is expected to increase significantly, employment for stock clerks is expected to decline through 2016, according to the U.S. Department of Labor. This is a result of increased automation and other productivity improvements that enable clerks to handle more stock. Manufacturing and wholesale trade industries are making the greatest use of automation. In addition to computerized inventory control systems, firms in these industries are expected to rely more on sophisticated conveyor belts, automatic high stackers to store and retrieve goods, and automatic guided vehicles that are battery powered and driverless. Sales floor stock clerks probably will be less affected by automation as most of their work is done on the sales floor, where it is difficult to locate or operate complicated machinery.

Because this occupation employs a large number of workers, many job openings will occur each year to replace stock clerks who transfer to other jobs and leave the labor force. Stock clerk jobs tend to be entry-level positions, so many vacancies will be created by normal career progression to other occupations.

FOR MORE INFORMATION

For information on educational programs in the retail industry, contact
National Retail Federation
325 7th Street, NW, Suite 1100
Washington, DC 20004-2818
Tel: 800-673-4692
http://www.nrf.com

Typists and Word Processors

OVERVIEW

Using typewriters, personal computers, and other office machines, *typists* and *word processors* convert handwritten or otherwise unfinished material into clean, readable, typewritten copies. Typists create reports, letters, forms, tables, charts, and other materials for all kinds of businesses and services. Word processors create the same types of materials using a computer and word processing software. Other typists use special machines that convert manuscripts into Braille, coded copy, or typeset copy. Typists and word processors hold about 179,000 jobs in the United States.

HISTORY

The invention of the typewriter in 1829 by W. A. Burt greatly increased business efficiency and productivity, and its benefits increased as typists became skilled at quickly transforming messy handwritten documents into neat, consistently typed copies.

More recently, the introduction of word processing into the workplace has revolutionized typing. This task may be done on a personal computer, a computer terminal hooked up to a network, or a computer that strictly handles word processing functions. Workers can correct errors and make any necessary changes right on the screen before a hard copy is printed on paper, thus eliminating the need for retyping whole pages to correct mistakes. The computer stores the information in

QUICK FACTS

School Subjects
Computer science
English

Personal Skills
Following instructions
Mechanical/manipulative

Work Environment
Primarily indoors
Primarily one location

Minimum Education Level
High school diploma

Salary Range
$20,920 to $30,380 to $44,780+

Certification or Licensing
None available

Outlook
Decline

DOT
203

GOE
09.09.01

NOC
1411

O*NET-SOC
43-9021.00, 43-9022.00

its memory, so the worker can go back to it again and again for copies or changes.

The term *word processing* entered the English language in 1965, when International Business Machines, more commonly known as IBM, introduced a typewriter that put information onto magnetic tape instead of paper. Corrections could be made on this tape before running the tape through a machine that converted the signals on the tape into characters on a printed page. Today, word processing software and personal computers have virtually replaced typewriters in the office.

THE JOB

Some typists perform few duties other than typing. These workers spend approximately 75 percent of their time at the keyboard. They may input statistical data, medical reports, legal briefs, addresses, letters, and other documents from handwritten copies. They may work in pools, dividing the work of a large office among many workers under the supervision of a typing section chief. These typists may also be responsible for making photocopies of typewritten materials for distribution.

Beginning typists may start by typing address labels, headings on form letters, and documents from legible handwritten copy. More experienced typists may work from copy that is more difficult to read or needs to be printed in tabular form.

Clerk-typists spend up to 50 percent of their time typing. They also perform a variety of clerical tasks such as filing, answering the phone, acting as receptionists, and operating copy machines.

Many typists type from audio recordings instead of written or printed copy. *Transcribing-machine operators* sit at keyboards and wear headsets, through which they hear the spoken contents of letters, reports, and meetings. Typists can control the speed of the recording so they can comfortably type every word they hear. They proofread their finished documents and may erase dictated recordings for future reuse. Some typists in this subspecialty pursue advanced education to become medical transcriptionists or court reporters.

Most common of the computer typists are word processors. These employees put documents into the proper format by entering codes into the word processing software, indicating which lines to center, which words to underline, where the margins should be set, and so forth, and how the document should be stored and printed. Word processors can edit, change, insert, and delete materials instantly by just pressing keys. Word processing is particularly efficient for form letters, in which only certain parts of a document change on each copy. When a word processor has finished formatting and keying in a document, it is electronically sent to a printer for a finished copy. The document is normally saved on a disk or the computer's hard drive so that any subsequent changes to it can be made easily and new copies produced immediately. Word processors also can send electronic files via email or modems to people in different locations.

Braille typists and *Braille operators* use special typewriter-like machines to transcribe written or spoken English into Braille. By pressing one key or a combination of keys, they create the raised characters of the Braille alphabet. They may print either on special paper or on metal plates, which are later used to print books or other publications.

REQUIREMENTS

High School
Most employers require that typists and word processors be high school graduates and able to type accurately at a rate of at least 40 or 50 words per minute. Typists need good knowledge of spelling, grammar, and punctuation and may be required to be familiar with standard office equipment.

Postsecondary Training
In addition to high schools, there are colleges, business schools, and home-study courses that teach keyboarding skills. Some people learn keyboarding through self-teaching materials such as books, recordings, and computer programs. Business schools and community colleges often offer certificates or associate's degrees for typists and word processors.

For those who do not pursue such formal education, temporary agencies will often train workers in these skills. Generally, it takes a minimum of three to six months of experience to become a skilled word processor.

Word processors must be able to type 45–80 words per minute and should know the proper way to organize such documents as letters, reports, and financial statements. Increasingly, employers are requiring that employees know how to use various software programs for word processing, spreadsheet, and database management tasks.

Other Requirements

To be a successful typist and word processor, you need manual dexterity and the ability to concentrate. You should be alert, efficient, and attentive to detail. Because you will often work directly with other people, you need good interpersonal skills, including a courteous and cheerful demeanor. Good listening skills are important in order to transcribe recorded material.

EXPLORING

As with many clerical occupations, a good way to gain experience as a typist is through high school work-study programs. Students in these programs work part time for local businesses and attend classes part time. Temporary agencies also provide training and temporary jobs for exploring the field. Another way to gain typing experience is to volunteer to type for friends, religious groups, or other organizations and to create your own computerized reports.

EMPLOYERS

Typists and word processors are employed in almost every kind of workplace, including banks, law firms, factories, schools, hospitals, publishing firms, department stores, and government agencies. They may work with groups of employees in large offices or with only one or two other people in small offices.

There are approximately 179,000 typists and word processors employed in the United States. About one-fifth of all data entry and information processing workers work in firms that provide business services, including temporary help, word processing, and computer and data processing. Approximately 15 percent work in state or local government agencies.

STARTING OUT

Business school and college students may learn of typing or word processing positions through their schools' career services offices. Some large businesses recruit employees directly from these schools. High school guidance counselors also may know of local job openings.

People interested in typing or word processor positions can check the want ads in newspapers and business journals for companies with job openings. They can apply directly to the personnel departments of large companies that hire many of these workers. They also can register with temporary agencies. To apply for positions with the federal government, job seekers should apply at the nearest regional Office of Personnel Management, or they can visit its Web site, http://www.usajobs.gov. State, county, and city governments may also have listings for such positions.

ADVANCEMENT

Typists and word processors usually receive salary increases as they gain experience and are promoted from junior to senior positions. These are often given a classification or pay scale designation, such as typist or word processor I or II. They may also advance from clerk-typist to technical typist, or from a job in a typing pool to a typing position in a private office.

A degree in business management or executive secretarial skills increases a typist's chances for advancement. In addition, many large companies and government agencies provide training programs that allow workers to upgrade their skills and move into other jobs, such as secretary, statistical clerk, or stenographer.

Once they have acquired enough experience, some typists and word processors go into business for themselves and provide typing services to business clients working from their homes. They may find work typing reports, manuscripts, and papers for professors, authors, business people, and students.

The more word processing experience an employee has, the better the opportunities to move up. Some may be promoted to word processing supervisor or selected for in-house professional training programs in data processing. Word processors may also move into related fields and work as word processing equipment salespeople or servicers, or word processing teachers or consultants.

EARNINGS

The U.S. Department of Labor reports that word processors and typists had median annual earnings of $30,380 in 2007. Salaries ranged from less than $20,920 to more than $44,780.

Typists and word processors occasionally may work overtime to finish special projects and may receive overtime pay. In large cities workers usually receive paid holidays, two weeks of vacation time after one year of employment, sick leave, health and life insurance, and a pension plan. Some large companies also provide dental insurance, profit sharing opportunities, and bonuses.

WORK ENVIRONMENT

Typists and word processors usually work 35–40 hours per week at workstations in clean, bright offices. They usually sit most of the day in a fairly small area. The work is detailed and often repetitious, and approaching deadlines may increase the pressure and demands placed on typists and word processors.

Recent years have seen a controversy develop concerning the effect that working at video display terminals (VDTs) can have on workers' health. Working with these screens in improper lighting can cause eyestrain, and sitting at a workstation all day can cause musculoskeletal stress and pain. The computer industry is paying closer attention to these problems and is working to improve health and safety standards in VDT-equipped offices.

Another common ailment for typists and word processors is carpal tunnel syndrome, a painful ailment of the tendons in the wrist that is triggered by repetitive movement. If left unchecked it can require corrective surgery. However, proper placement of the typing keyboard can help prevent injury. Several companies have designed desks, chairs, and working spaces that accommodate the physical needs of typists and word processors in the best manner currently known.

The nature of this work lends itself to flexible work arrangements. Many typists and word processors work in temporary positions that provide flexible schedules. About 20 percent work part time. Some offices allow word processors and typists to telecommute from home, whereby they receive and send work on home computers via modems. These jobs may be especially convenient for workers with disabilities or family responsibilities, but often they do not provide a full range of benefits and lack the advantages of social interaction on the job.

OUTLOOK

Employment in the typing field is expected to decline over the next several years due to the increasing automation of offices. However, the sheer size of the occupation means that many jobs will become available for typists and word processors, especially to replace those employees who change careers or leave the workforce.

Technological innovations such as scanners, voice-recognition software, and electronic data transmission are being used in more workplaces, reducing the need for typists and word processors. Many office workers now do their own word processing because word processing and data entry software has become so user-friendly.

More companies today are outsourcing their data entry and word processing projects to temporary-help and staffing services firms. Most openings will be with these types of firms, and jobs will go to workers who have the best technical skills and knowledge of several word processing programs.

FOR MORE INFORMATION

For industry information, contact
International Association of Administrative Professionals
PO Box 20404
Kansas City, MO 64195-0404
Tel: 816-891-6600
Email: service@iaap-hq.org
http://www.iaap-hq.org

Index

Entries and page numbers in **bold**
indicate major treatment of a topic.

A

Abernathy, Julie 58, 64
academic library technicians 69
ACA International 20, 22
accountants
  bookkeeping and accounting clerks
  12
  railroads 113
account information clerks 13
accounting clerks. *See* bookkeeping
  and accounting clerks
accounts adjustable clerks (railroads)
  113
acquisitions technicians (library
  technicians) 68
actuarial clerks 142
administrative assistants. *See* medical
  secretaries; secretaries
administrative clerks 106
administrative secretaries 132
Advancement section, explained 3
advertising statistical clerks 141
agent-contract clerks 52
AHDI. *See* Association for
  Healthcare Documentation Integrity
  (AHDI)
AHIMA. *See* American Health
  Information Management
  Association (AHIMA)
American Academy of Professional
  Coders 85
American Bankers Association 37
American Federation of State,
  County, and Municipal Employees
  14
American Health Information
  Management Association (AHIMA)
  85–87
American Hotel & Lodging
  Educational Institute
  Lodging Management Program 45
American Institute of Banking 35, 37
American Institute of Professional
  Bookkeepers 13

American Library Association 68
American Medical Association
  Commission on Accreditation for
  Health Information Management
  Education 85
Association for Healthcare
  Documentation Integrity (AHDI)
  96, 98–99, 101
Association of American Railroads
  114, 117
Association of Credit and Collection
  Professionals 20
audit clerks 13
audit clerk supervisors 13

B

Bacon, David 133
Ballard Spahr Andrews & Ingersoll
  63–66
Bank Administration Institute 37, 40
bank loan officers 23
Bank of Massachusetts 32
Bank of North America 32
Bentley College of Healthcare
  Documentation 96
Best Western Golden Buff Lodge 47
bill collectors. *See* collection workers
billing clerks 5–10
  advancement 8–9
  billing-control clerks 7
  billing-machine operators 7
  COD (cash-on-delivery) clerks 7
  deposit-refund clerks 7
  earnings 9
  educational requirements 7
  employers 8
  employment outlook 9–10
  exploring the field 8
  foreign clerks 7
  high school requirements 7
  history 5–6
  information on 10
  interline clerks 7
  inventory-control clerks 7
  job, described 6–7
  passenger rate clerks 7
  postsecondary training 7

rate reviewers 7
raters 7
real estate 120
requirements 7–8
services clerks 7
settlement clerks 7
starting out 8
telegraph service raters 7
work environment 9
billing-control clerks 7
billing-machine operators 7
billing rate clerks 13
bookkeepers. *See also* bookkeeping
  and accounting clerks
  counter and retail clerks 34
  railroads 113
**bookkeeping and accounting clerks
  11–17**
  account information clerks 13
  advancement 15–16
  audit clerks 13
  audit clerks supervisors 13
  billing rate clerks 13
  certification or licensing 13–14
  earnings 14, 16
  educational requirements 13
  employers 15
  employment and earnings by
    industry 14
  employment outlook 16–17
  exploring the field 14–15
  fixed capital clerks 13
  general bookkeepers 12–13
  general-ledger bookkeepers
    12–13
  high school requirements 13
  history 11–12
  information on 17
  job, described 12–13
  organizations 13–14
  postsecondary training 13
  requirements 13–14
  starting out 15
  work environment 16
bookkeeping clerks
  counter and retail clerks 34
  real estate 120
Braille operators 155
Braille typists 155
Bunting, Marylou 100, 101

Burlington Northern Santa Fe
  Railroad 115
Burt, W. A. 153

C

cancellation clerks 52
Carnegie, Andrew 67
catalogers (library technicians) 68
Central Pacific Railroad 111
chart calculators 141
chart changers 141
chart clerks 141
children's library technicians 69
circulation counter attendants
  (library technicians) 68
claims clerks 51
claims examiners 51
claims supervisors 51
classifiers (library technicians) 68
clerk-typists 154
COD (cash-on-delivery) clerks 7
collateral-and-safekeeping clerks 34
collection agents. *See* collection
  workers
collection and exchange tellers 33
collection clerks 33
collection correspondents. *See*
  collection workers
collection workers 18–24
  advancement 22–23
  bank loan officers 23
  certification or licensing 21
  credit authorizers 23
  credit checkers 23
  credit investigators 23
  credit reporters 23
  earnings 23
  educational requirements 20
  employers 21–22
  employment outlook 24
  exploring the field 21
  facts about collections 22
  high school requirements 20
  history 18–19
  information on 24
  job, described 19–20
  organizations 20–22
  postsecondary training 20
  repossessors 19–20
  requirements 20–21

skip tracers 20
starting out 22
work environment 23–24
commodity-loan clerks 33
compilers 141
concrete products dispatchers 106
congressional-district aides 106
control clerks 34
counter and retail clerks 25–30
advancement 28–29
certification or licensing 27
earnings 29
educational requirements 27
employers 28
employment outlook 30
exploring the field 28
high school requirements 27
history 25
information on 30
job, described 26–27
organizations 27
rental car agents 27
requirements 27–28
service-establishment attendants 26
starting out 28
video-rental clerks 26
watch-and-clock repair clerks 26
work environment 29
credit authorizers 23
credit checkers 23
credit investigators 23
credit reporters 23
CSX Railroad 115

D
data abstractors 84
data analysts 84
decline, explained 3
demurrage clerks (railroads) 113
deposit-refund clerks 7
Dickens, Charles 18
Dictionary of Occupational Titles
(DOT) 2
discount tellers 33
dispatcher clerks 112
documentation-billing clerks 112–113

E
Earnings section, explained 3
Edison, Thomas A. 95

education secretaries 133, 134
Employers section, explained 3
encoder operators 34
executive assistants. *See* medical
secretaries
executive secretaries 134
Exploring section, explained 3
express clerks (railroads) 113

F
Ferguson's *Encyclopedia of Careers
and Vocational Guidance* 2
file clerks (real estate) 119–120
**financial institution tellers, clerks,
and related workers 31–41**
advancement 37–38
bookkeepers 34
bookkeeping clerks 34
collateral-and-safekeeping clerks
34
collection and exchange tellers 33
collection clerks 33
commercial tellers 31
commodity-loan clerks 33
control clerks 34
discount tellers 33
earnings 38
educational requirements 34–35
employers 36
employment outlook 39
encoder operators 34
exploring the field 36
foreign banknote tellers 33
head tellers 33
high school requirements 34–35
history 31–42
information on 39–40
interest clerks 34
interview 40–41
job, described 32–34
letter-of-credit clerks 34
messengers 34
note tellers 33
organizations 35, 37
pages 34
paying and receiving tellers 32
postsecondary training 35
proof machine operators 34
requirements 34–36
reserves clerks 34

starting out 37
statement clerks 34
teller supervisors 33
trust-mail clerks 34
wire-transfer clerks 34
work environment 38–39
fixed capital clerks 13
floaters (legal secretaries) 62
foreign banknote tellers 33
foreign clerks 7
For More Information section,
 explained 3
front office workers 43

G
Garland, Rebecca 59–60
general bookkeepers 12–13
general-ledger bookkeepers 12–13
The Grammar of Science (Pearson)
 140
Greenberg, Jeff 27, 43
Gregg, John Robert 131
growth, explained 3
Guide for Occupational Exploration
 (GOE) 2

H
Haynes and Boone, LLP 58
head tellers 33
Health Data Matrix 100
History section, explained 3
Holiday Inn 42
hotel desk clerks 42–49
advancement 47
certification or licensing 45–46
earnings 47
educational requirements 45
employers 46–47
employment outlook 48
exploring the field 46
front office workers 43
high school requirements 45
history 42–43
information on 48–49
job, described 43–45
organizations 45
postsecondary training 45
requirements 45–46
reservation clerks 43
starting out 47

U.S. lodging industry, facts (2007)
 44
work environment 48
Hoteljobs.com 47
Human Resources Development
 Canada 2

I
IBM. *See* International Business
 Machines (IBM)
Infanti, Patricia 61, 63–66
information clerks. *See* receptionists
information on, explained 3
insurance agents 51
insurance brokers 51
insurance checkers 52
**insurance policy processing workers
 50–56**
advancement 54
agent-contract clerks 52
cancellation clerks 52
claims clerks 51
claims examiners 51
claims supervisors 51
earnings 54–55
educational requirements 53
employers 54
employment outlook 55
exploring the field 53
high school requirements 53
history 50–51
information on 55–56
insurance agents 51
insurance brokers 51
insurance checkers 52
job, described 51–52
medical-voucher clerks 52
policy-change clerks 51–52
postsecondary training 53
requirements 53
reviewers 51
revival clerks 52
starting out 54
work environment 55
interest clerks 34
interline clerks 7, 113
International Association of
 Administrative Professionals
 medical secretaries 92
 office clerks 106

real estate clerks 120
secretaries 135
International Business Machines
(IBM) 154
International Union of Electronic,
Electrical, Salaried, Machine and
Furniture Workers-Communications
Workers of America 14
interviews
counter and financial institution
tellers, clerk, and related workers
40–41
legal secretaries 64–66
library technicians 77–78
inventory clerks 147
inventory-control clerks 7

J
JIST Works 2
Job section, explained 3

K
kitchen clerks 148

L
Legacy Bank 40–41
legal secretaries 57–66
advancement 62
certification or licensing
60–61
earnings 62–63
employers 61–62
employment outlook 63–64
exploring the field 61
floaters 62
high school requirements 60
history 57–58
information on 64
interview 64–66
job, described 58–59
organizations 60–61
postsecondary training 60
requirements 60–61
starting out 62
work environment 63
Legal Secretaries International 61
letter-of-credit clerks 34
Library of Congress 72
library technical assistants. *See*
library technicians

library technicians 67–78
academic library technicians 69
acquisitions technicians 68
advancement 73–74
catalogers 68
children's library technicians 69
circulation counter attendants 68
classifiers 68
earnings 74
educational requirements 70–71
employers 72
employment outlook 75
exploring the field 72
high school requirements 70
history 67–68
information on 75–76
interview 77–78
job, described 68–70
library facts 70
media technicians 68
organizations 68
reference library technicians 69
requirements 70–72
school library media specialists 69
school library technicians 69
starting out 73
work environment 74–75
young-adult library technicians 69
linen room attendants 148
litigation secretaries. *See* legal
secretaries
London, University of 140

M
magazine keepers 148
MarketData Enterprises 22
Martindill, Robin 77–78
material clerks 147
Mayo Medical Clinic 92
media technicians 68
medical language specialists. *See*
medical transcriptionists
medical record technicians 79–89,
141
advancement 87
certification or licensing 85
data abstractors 84
data analysts 84
earnings 87–88
educational requirements 84–85

employers 86
employment outlook 88–89
exploring the field 86
high school requirements 84
history 79–81
information on 89
job, described 81–84
organizations 85, 86
postsecondary training 85
requirements 84–86
starting out 86–87
statistical clerks 141
statistical technicians 141
work environment 88
medical secretaries 90–94, 133
advancement 93
certification or licensing 92
earnings 93
educational requirements 91–92
employers 92
employment outlook 93–94
exploring the field 92
high school requirements 91
history 90
information on 94
job, described 91
learn more about it 91
organizations 92
postsecondary training 92
requirements 91–92
starting out 93
work environment 93
medical stenographers. *See* medical
transcriptionists
medical transcribers. *See* medical
transcriptionists
medical transcriptionists 95–104
advancement 101
certification or licensing 99
earnings 101–102
educational requirements 98–99
employers 100
employment outlook 102–103
exploring the field 100
high school requirements 98
history 95–96
information on 103–104
job, described 96–98
organizations 96, 98–99
portrait of, 2007 96

postsecondary training 98–99
requirements 98–100
starting out 101
work environment 102
medical-voucher clerks 52
membership secretaries 134
merchandise distributors 147
Merchant of Venice (Shakespeare) 18
messengers 34
metal control coordinators 148
Money magazine 36
Montgomery, Alexis 58–60, 62

N
NALS...the association for legal pro-
fessionals 60, 135
National Association of Credit
Management 20
National Occupational Classification
(NOC) Index 2
National Retail Federation 27
Norfolk Southern Railroad 115
note tellers 33

O
Occupational Information Network
(O*NET)-Standard Occupational
Classification System (SOC) Index
2
Occupational Outlook Handbook
generally 3
hotel desk clerks 48
legal secretaries 64
receptionists 129
Office and Professional Employees
International Union 14
office clerks 105–110
administrative clerks 106
advancement 108
certification or licensing 107
concrete products dispatchers 106
congressional-district aides 106
earnings 108–109
educational requirements 107
employers 107–108
employment outlook 109
exploring the field 107
high school requirements 107
history 105–106
information on 109–110

job, described 106
organizations 107
police clerks 106
postsecondary training 107
requirements 107
starting out 108
work environment 109
office coordinators. *See* medical secretaries
office managers. *See* medical secretaries
Office of Personnel Management 147
OfficeTeam 1, 109
operators of business and computing machines (railroads) 113
order fillers 147
Outlook section, explained 3
Overview section, explained 3

P

pages 34
parts clerks 148
parts order and stock clerks 148
passenger rate clerks 7
paying and receiving tellers 32
Pearson, Karl 140
personal secretaries 134
Physicians' Desk Reference 100
Pitman, Isaac 131
police clerks 106
policy-change clerks 51–52
Poole's Index to Periodical Literature 68
prescription clerks 148
PricewaterhouseCoopers 22
property custodians 148

Q

Quick Facts section, explained 2

R

railroad clerks 111–117
accountants 113
accounts adjustable clerks 113
advancement 115–116
bookkeepers 113
demurrage clerks 113
did you know? 113
dispatcher clerks 112

documentation-billing clerks 112–113
earnings 116
educational requirements 114
employers 115
employment outlook 117
exploring the field 115
express clerks 113
high school requirements 114
history 111–112
information on 117
interline clerks 113
job, described 112–113
operators of business and computing machines 113
organizations 114, 116, 117
postsecondary training 114
railroad-maintenance clerks 112
records and statistics clerks 113
requirements 114–115
revising clerks 113
secretaries 113
starting out 115
stenographers 113
top freight revenue by commodity, 2007 114
train clerks 112
typists 113
voucher clerks 113
work environment 116–117
yard clerks 112
railroad-maintenance clerks 112
rate reviewers 7
raters 7
real estate clerks 118–123
advancement 121
billing clerks 120
bookkeeping clerks 120
certification or licensing 120
earnings 121
educational requirements 120
employers 121
employment outlook 122
exploring the field 120–121
file clerks 119–120
high school requirements 120
history 118
information on 122–123
job, described 118–120
organizations 120

postsecondary training 120
requirements 120
starting out 121
work environment 121–122
receptionists 124–130
advancement 128
earnings 129
educational requirements 126–127
employers 128
employment outlook 129
exploring the field 128
high school requirements 126
history 124–125
information on 130
job, described 125–126
postsecondary training 126–127
requirements 126–128
starting out 128
switchboard operators 124–126
work environment 129
records and statistics clerks (railroads) 113
reference library technicians 69
rental car agents 27
repossessors 19–20
Requirements section, explained 3
reservation clerks 43
reserves clerks 34
retail clerks. *See* counter and retail
clerks
reviewers 51
revising clerks (railroads) 113
revival clerks 52
Rietcheck, Lucinda 40–41

S
Salary.com 121
San Diego Mesa College 77–78
Sarbanes-Oxley Act of 2002 16
school library media specialists 69
school library technicians 69
secretaries 131–139
administrative secretaries 132
advancement 137
certification or licensing 135
earnings 137
educational requirements 134–135
education secretaries 133, 134
employers 136

employment outlook 138
executive secretaries 134
exploring the field 136
high school requirements 134
history 131–132
information on 139
job, described 132–134
legal secretaries. *See* legal
secretaries
medical secretaries. *See* medical
secretaries
membership secretaries 134
organizations 135
personal secretaries 134
postsecondary training 134–135
railroads 113
requirements 134–136
responsibilities and career prospects 135
social secretaries 134
starting out 136–137
technical secretaries 133–134
work environment 138
service-establishment attendants 26
services clerks 7
settlement clerks 7
Shakespeare, William 18
Sheffert, Terrence 19, 21–23
Sheraton Manhattan 46
shipping and receiving clerks 147
skip tracers 20
social secretaries 134
space and storage clerks 148
Starting Out section, explained 3
statement clerks 34
statistical clerks 140–145
actuarial clerks 142
advancement 143
advertising statistical clerks 141
chart calculators 141
chart changers 141
chart clerks 141
compilers 141
earnings 144
educational requirements 142
employers 143
employment outlook 144
exploring the field 142–143
high school requirements 142

history 140–141
information on 144–145
job, described 141–142
medical records clerks and
  technicians 141
postsecondary training 142
requirements 142
starting out 143
work environment 144
Statler Hotels 42
stenographers (railroads) 113
Stephenson, George 111
stock clerks 146–152
advancement 150–151
earnings 148, 151
educational requirements 149
employers 150
employment 148
employment outlook 152
exploring the field 150
high school requirements 149
history 146
information on 152
inventory clerks 147
job, described 146–149
kitchen clerks 148
linen room attendants 148
magazine keepers 148
material clerks 147
merchandise distributors 147
metal control coordinators 148
order fillers 147
parts clerks 148
parts order and stock clerks 148
prescription clerks 148
property custodians 148
requirements 149
shipping and receiving clerks
  147
space and storage clerks 148
starting out 150
stock-control clerks 147
storekeepers 149
tool crib attendants 148
work environment 151
stock-control clerks 147
storekeepers 149
Stulberg, Scott 80, 127
switchboard operators 124–126

T

technical secretaries 133–134
telegraph service raters 7
tellers. *See* financial institution tellers,
  clerk, and related workers
teller supervisors 33
tool crib attendants 148
top freight revenue by commodity,
  2007 114
train clerks 112
transcribing-machine operators 154
Transportation Communications
  Union 116
Trevithick, Richard 111
trial secretaries. *See* legal secretaries
trust-mail clerks 34
**typists and word processors
153–159**
advancement 157
Braille operators 155
Braille typists 155
clerk-typists 154
earnings 157
educational requirements 155
employers 156
employment outlook 158–159
exploring the field 156
high school requirements 155
history 153–154
information on 159
job, described 154–155
postsecondary training 155
railroads 113
requirements 155–156
starting out 156–157
transcribing-machine operators
  154
word processors, described
  154–155
work environment 158

U

Union Pacific Railroad 111, 115
U.S. Bureau of Labor Statistics 3
U.S. Department of Agriculture 143
U.S. Department of Commerce 143
U.S. Department of Defense 72
U.S. Department of Health and
  Human Services 143

U.S. Department of Labor
  billing clerks 9
  bookkeeping and accounting clerks
    15–17
  collection workers 23–24
  counter and financial institution
    tellers, clerk, and related workers
    38–39
  counter and retail clerks 29–30
  generally 2
  hotel desk clerks 47
  insurance policy processing
    workers 54–55
  legal secretaries 62–63
  library technicians 74–75
  medical record technicians 87,
    88
  medical secretaries 93
  medical transcriptionists
    102–103
  office clerks 108
  railroad clerks 116
  receptionists 128, 129
  secretaries 137, 138
  statistical clerks 144

  stock clerks 148, 151, 152
  typists and word processors 157
U.S. lodging industry, facts (2007)
  44
U.S. Railroad Retirement
  Administration 116

V

video-rental clerks 26
voucher clerks (railroads) 113

W

watch-and-clock repair clerks 26
West, Jim 149
wire-transfer clerks 34
Witry, Lynda 45–46
word processors. *See* typists and
  word processors
Work Environment section, explained
  3

Y

yard clerks 112
YMCA 71
young-adult library technicians 69